BAILOUT CONSPIRACY

They Stole Your Money

BAILOUT CONSPIRACY

They Stole Your Money

Frank Latell

My appreciation to Jill Yris, editor;

without her this book would not exist in its present form.

"If you tell the truth,
you don't have to remember anything."

Attributed to Mark Twain, 1894

Table of Contents

ONE HUNDRED SIXTEEN BILLION, ONE HUNDRED

and

49 MILLION DOLLARS

you have been robbed

Introduction

Let me tell you a story about a crook, a lawyer and a giant.

"Fatto un torto," I say. "Peter Triano, the loan servicer, Lawrence Rochefort, the foreclosure attorney, and Fannie Mae have all done me wrong and thinking back to my Italian heritage, I imagined taking revenge.

"Being that I thought murder would not go well with God, I imagined a gunshot in each of Triano's knees and one elbow would be suitable. I thought that leaving one good arm would be justified, in that it would not be fair for someone else to have to wipe his stronzo!"

My true crime story reveals a scheme of entrapment to default as a requirement for loan modification, which includes deceit, foreclosure of properties, stealing of government tax money, the suspicious death of a key witness, a Federal Court Summary Judgment and finding the smoking gun.

Each chapter takes you on a roller-coaster journey involving a major theft from the U. S. Treasury, a trial and our government, who makes laws regarding taxpayer money, creates an agency to oversee the requirements of spending that money, a bureau responsible for consumer protection and an existing department responsible for investigating crimes against the government, who all failed in their reason to exist.

My documented story will prove - every step of the way – how the money trail leads to fraud. How a conspiracy is stealing from me – and from you.

(Fig. 1)

AFFIDAVIT OF FRANK LATELL

STATE OF FLORIDA
COUNTY OF LEE

BEFORE ME, the undersigned authority, personally appeared, FRANK LATELL, who sworn, on oath, deposes and says of his personal knowledge, as follows:

1. I, FRANK LATELL, am a resident of Lee County, Florida, and I am over the age of eighteen.

2. Everything that has been written in my non-fiction novel, "THEY STOLE YOUR MONEY" previously titled "KILL FANNIE MAE" is the truth, to the best of my knowledge and recollection.

3. My attorney, Matthew Toll, has reviewed this book to ensure that the contents do not contain anything that could be construed as a "technical untruth."

4. No libelous statements have been made. "Truth is an absolute defense to any claim for defamation."

5. If I die under suspicious conditions following the publication of this book, I request a full and legitimate homicide investigation.

FURTHER AFFIANT SAYETH NAUGHT.

FRANK LATELL

Sworn to (or affirmed) and subscribed before me on this 7th day of July, 2020, by FRANK LATELL, who is personally known to me.

MATTHEW TOLL
Notary Public - State of Florida
Commission # GG 059139
My Comm. Expires Feb 18, 2021
Bonded through National Notary Assn.

NOTARY PUBLIC

3

Chapter 1: Crisis

During World War II, a former Royal Air Force station was active in Scotland 4 miles from the small village of Edzell. With Georgia-era architecture, the town had a castle, church and just over the North Esk river, the airfield. In the 1960's, the U.S. Navy Global High Frequency Direction Finding (HFDF) network at RAF Edzell was used to track various targets around the world.

As a young man, during my fifth and senior year as a part-time student in college, I needed nine credit hours to graduate. But our government decided to draft me into the army; instead, I quickly enrolled for three more credit hours to qualify as a full-time student, which effectively extended the draft until graduation. I then eliminated the draft by volunteering for officer candidate school in the U.S. Navy.

As a commissioned naval officer, I was assigned to the U.S. Naval Air Station in Chincoteague, Virginia and Mobile Construction Battalions 6 and 8. I was reassigned to RAF Edzell, in Angus, Scotland, UK, a strategic move that changed my life.

As a youngster growing up in Girard, Ohio, I knew what it was like to earn your way through work. At a young age I went with my older brother delivering the local newspaper and then worked for a fruit and vegetable huckster yelling "water-ma-lon-ne" from the back of his truck in the local neighborhoods. A little older I got a job through my father as a shoeshine boy at a hat blocking and shoeshine parlor, men liked their hats and shoes looking good, in downtown Youngstown. I would ride the bus from Girard to the Youngstown bus terminal and walk to the city square. On Saturdays, after shining shoes all day, I had a hard time keeping my pants up from my pockets filled with all the coins I had from tips. I wore a non-tuck long shirt to cover my bulging pockets in fear of older kids seeing the bulge and stealing from me. Later, I worked as an usher in the local movie theater and then in a lumber yard. During my senior year in high school, after a full day of school, I worked in the steel mill from 4 to midnight.

During my high school and college years, I was living with my mom, dad and brothers. Out in our backyard was a chicken coop that I used as a workshop. Fortunately, there was a partition between my shop and the chickens. I was fascinated by building things and in my spare time, I built 3 boats. The first was a flat bottom row boat that extended but fit in the back of a pick-up truck. The second was a canoe, which we carried on the top of a vehicle. I then purchased and assembled a 'kit' boat. I built a trailer and purchased a second-hand Scott Atwater 16 horsepower boat motor and on weekends we would be off to Mosquito Lake fishing and water skiing.

I went to nearby Youngstown College, William Rayen School of Engineering, in pursuit of a civil engineering degree. I attended mostly night school working days as a land surveyor for Trumbull County, Ohio. I then worked as a structural draftsman for the Ohio Steel Corporation. On Saturdays I worked checking fabrication drawings for a structural steel engineer. I paid for my car, my college education and contributed to the home expenses.

My older brother joined the Navy right out of high school but I remember one time when my brother's ship was in port, my dad and brother only showed me the ugliest parts of The USS Yellowstone, a destroyer tender. Their plan of discouraging me from joining the Navy back-fired because I liked the ship and camaraderie between the officers.

While serving in Edzell, I met a girl named Kathleen Swan. Kathleen, or Kit as I called her, was a recent graduate from Stracathro Hospital and Nursing School in Angus, and a registered nurse. She was beautiful and I said to myself, *this is the girl I am going to marry*.

Six weeks after a Scottish wedding, I was transferred to U.S. Naval Air Station New Orleans, Louisiana as the Publics Works Officer. Kit took a job working for a doctor, made a home for us and enjoyed being a naval officer's wife.

Leaving the U.S. Navy in 1964, we went to my home in Girard. I became a licensed professional engineer and general contractor. We started a family and I began building multi-family rental apartments.

In 1971, we sold our share of ownership in the brothers owned family rental properties and moved to Fort Myers, Florida. I designed and built other multi-family rental apartment complexes keeping 113 units in the Croix and Peppertree apartments. We managed all units at maximum occupancy and they were providing us with generous cash flow. Our intentions were to keep these properties for our retirement income. I worked hard all my life, but nothing prepared me for a devious, money-making crime against me.

(Fig. 2)

In 2006, many Americans had subprime home mortgages with an interest rate that increased over time and then in 2007, real estate prices began to collapse throughout the US and the world. In Washington, the Federal Reserve and other agencies of the US Government responded to the crisis by flooding the market with money, reducing the interest rate and increasing spending to provide Government assistance.

I remember the Lehman Brothers, a global financial service company that operated for 158 years and was the 4th largest investment bank in the US with $600 billion in assets. In 2008, Lehman Brothers filed for bankruptcy, the largest in our history. The Dow Jones dropped over 500 points and panic ensued and led to a full-fledged financial panic by the fall of 2008. What followed was the most serious recession since the Great Depression of the 1930s.

Lehman Brothers, via JPMorgan Chase, was given Federal

Reserve-backed advances of $138 million. While this was happening, keep in mind that Richard Fuld, a Lehman Brothers executive, was paid over an 8-year timeframe the staggering amount of $300 million.

During this traumatic period, the great state of Florida was especially hard-hit.

Personally, some of my tenants lost their jobs and were unable to pay their rent. Due to eviction notices, a few tenants kicked holes in the walls and left their units a mess. After I saw what happened, I replaced management, and alongside my crew, ripped up carpets and replaced them with tile, patched and painted walls and went to work on renovating our units.

One of the Government's programs to battle the financial panic was the Treasury's rescue of Fannie Mae and other lending institutions pursuant to the authority created by the Housing Economic Recovery Act of 2008.

The Housing and Economic Recovery Act, enacted July 30, 2008, commonly referred to as "HERA," was designed primarily to address the subprime mortgage crisis. It was intended to restore confidence in Fannie Mae and Freddie Mac by strengthening regulations and injecting capital into the two large U.S. suppliers of housing mortgage funding.

HERA changed many laws that affected both the housing and mortgage markets. Included in the act were provisions to strengthen and unify oversight of the housing Government Sponsored Enterprises (GSEs), such as Fannie Mae, Freddie Mac and the Federal Home Loan Banks. The Treasury was authorized to lend or invest an unlimited amount of money in any of the regulated entities in the event of financial or mortgage market emergencies.

At the time, Fannie Mae and Freddie Mac faced a series of accounting and financial problems, which led many in Congress to conclude that there was a need for a stronger regulator. HERA created the Federal Housing Finance Agency (FHFA) to be the new regulator for the housing GSEs.

The Housing and Economic Recovery Act gives the Federal Housing Finance Agency (FHFA) broad authority to regulate the housing GSEs. FHFA was granted the authority to take over and reorganize an insolvent Fannie Mae and Freddie Mac. This authority was used on September 7, 2008 when the FHFA placed Fannie Mae and Freddie Mac under conservatorship.

Conservatorship means being responsible for someone who is unable to take care of their responsibilities - or is just plain incompetent.

Chapter 2: Deception

Ironically, thanks to the US Treasury bailout, Fannie Mae made money by foreclosing on properties, which was obviously not the intent of the Housing and Economic Recovery Act and the subsequent conservatorship.

When my wife and I signed up for 10-year balloon Fannie Mae loans, little did we know that we would be falling into a deep, black hole of aggravation, embarrassment and financial loss.

The Fannie Mae loans on our properties originated September 14, 2005 through Independence Community Bank, a banking corporation, organized and existing under the state of New York. Independence Community Bank was the servicer of our Fannie loans. On or about September 9, 2006, Independence Community Bank was acquired by Sovereign Bank who simultaneously became a financial partner with Grupo Santander. As a result, Sovereign/Santander National Bank became the servicer of our loans.

Prior to late 2006, multi-family rental housing in Southwest Florida was being bought, converted and sold as condominiums, with huge profits. Lending institutions, including Fannie Mae, provided overvalued loans on these properties. Due to the housing crash of 2007, the value of these over-mortgaged properties had greatly declined and were in great financial stress. Although we did not refinance, we experienced the effects of loss of tenants and lower rents.

For three years, we put any available funds back into our properties. A small amount of additional money, other than the rents being generated by the apartments, had to be invested to meet the costs of rehabbing the units. Fortunately, we were not over-mortgaged as other similar properties. Just prior to the housing crash, offers to buy our properties for conversion into the condominium market were tempting; we chose to keep our properties in a market, which was soon to become a market with a shortage of rental properties. When the housing crash occurred, although rentals suffered due to the job loss, we were not incumbered with part condominium and part rental properties and being over financed.

In 2010, the commercial loan interest rates available in the open market were considerably lower than the rates we were paying on our Croix and Peppertree loans. We investigated and found that multi-family loans could be refinanced through loan modifications at three, plus or minus, percent interest rate for qualified candidates of excellent creditworthiness; we would have qualified.

***

At this time, there were three names that you should remember: Lyle Preest, Peter Triano and Lawrence Rochefort.

Preest, a friend who was also a financial professional, was appointed as the Finance Officer of our Latell properties, and in this capacity, he sought to seek a modification of the interest rates associated with the loans. He attempted to make contact with the Fannie Mae loan servicer, a Sovereign Bank loan workout officer, Peter Triano.

According to Preest, Sovereign Bank could not discuss a loan modification or workout if the loans in question were not in default or over 45 days past due. In other words, loan modifications were only available to those who had defaulted, not those who were current in their obligations.

Peter Triano had transferred from Independence Community Bank to Sovereign Bank. At the time of my attempt to get a Fannie Mae loan rate modification, Triano was the Sovereign Bank Vice-President, Debt Management & Recovery Workout Officer.

Preest was eventually referred to the Fannie Mae attorney, Lawrence Rochefort, whose resume stated that he was a representative of Sovereign Bank in foreclosure of income producing commercial properties.

One of these three men will end up dead.

Chapter 3: Stealthy Foreclosure

I just wanted a lower interest rate. And I knew the rental market in Florida since the early 70s and wasn't worried about losing the apartments. Other people were selling their rental properties and I was the exception because I wanted to keep my properties.

In April 2010, my financial officer Preest notified Sovereign bank that the decreased cash flow associated with reduced rents, combined with the increasing renovation expenses, were factors making it difficult - if not impossible - to make the required loan payments solely from the cash flow generated by the apartments. Two certified letters and several phone calls were made by Preest without response.

Lawrence Rochefort, the guy who represented Fannie Mae, was an attorney with Akerman, Senterfitt, LLP. In October, he secretly started foreclosure actions against our property loans. The next month, he sent me a certified letter that stated they were accelerating the full amount of our apartment loans and that if indebtedness was not immediately paid, I may elect to pursue any and all remedies available, including foreclosure. In my world, I'd call that two-faced!

For eight months, from April 2010 through November 2010, I had directed Andrew Bethke, from our management company, to give me the exact to the penny amount of the monthly mortgage payments. I had kept these funds handy so that they would immediately be available for the anticipated loan modification agreements.

And we did not need to default. I could afford to make the mortgage payments and costs of the rehabilitations. We defaulted because we were explicitly advised that defaulting was the only way to obtain - or even be considered for - loan modifications.

Up until this time, I had relied on my finance officer to handle negotiations for getting a lower interest rate. It appears that he was being played for a fool. Now looking back, I should have spotted the scheme. Mortgage loan officer Triano, never available now, was making our contact through the bank attorney.

Knowing Fannie Mae's required loan servicing procedures that we requested and they kept hidden from us, made me angry. I assumed that they had a lot of practice pulling this scheme on other S.W. Florida Fannie Mae financed property owners, but these owners were in over their heads in debt. Our properties were a different situation (explained later), and I assumed Triano got in too deep with our properties and Santander could not back down.

Now, my feeling is that Fannie Mae's initiation of foreclosures, while we were in the midst of good faith negotiations, was akin to the U.S. at peace while in the middle of negotiations with the Japanese Empire - and their sudden and deliberate attack on Pearl Harbor!

Chapter 4: Misinterpretation

After eight months of trying to make contact with the Fannie Mae loan service workout officer, we acted with a QWR, a Qualified Written Request. Fannie Mae's loan officer had turned into a collective Scarlet Pimpernel. As Sir Percy's character, played by actor Leslie Howard, said in the 1934 movie, "They seek him here, they seek him there…is he in heaven or is he in hell? That damned elusive Pimpernel!"

If there is a place with fire and brimstone, you can bet your bottom dollar that the Fannie Mae guy will be there.

***

The Real Estate Settlement Procedures Act (RESPA) was primarily designed to ensure that consumers in real estate transactions received timely information about the costs of the settlement process. RESPA also imposed certain requirements on loan servicer's, such as correcting errors or answering a QWR, which is a request for information that you, or someone acting on your behalf, can send to your mortgage servicer.

On November 26, 2010, a Qualified Written Request was sent via certified mail to Mr. Peter C. Triano, VP – Workout Center, Sovereign Bank as follows:

"We dispute the amount you allege is owed as per the latest

billing statement on the loan. We also dispute whether you have the legal authority to collect on this loan as we have not been provided proof that you either are the holder of the note and mortgages or you have been appointed the servicing agent by the holder of the note. Furthermore, we dispute that the company that alleges it holds the note and mortgage is the actual holder of said note.

"We have previously requested this information months ago through our approved representative, CFO Services, from your collections department, but only received an apology for many errors in your demand letter and the acknowledgement that Sovereign Bank cannot provide a certified copy of the original note executed by the borrower. None of the items requested were ever forwarded to us. Consider this a qualified written request pursuant to the Real Estate Settlement Procedures Act Section 2605(e)."

The letter went on to request specific items:

"We are attempting to assess our financial position on this investment as we wish to keep this asset, as we have not abandoned the property. Hopefully, once the required information is received and reviewed, we wish to discuss a loan modification with the note holder/qualified servicer."

Signed by Lyle W. Preest, Chief Financial Officer
and Frank A. Latell, President.

The QWR was obviously forwarded to the legal firm of Akerman, Senterfitt with the following response dated December 16, 2010:

"This firm represents Fannie Mae, the holder of the above referred loan. This letter is written on behalf of Fannie Mae and Sovereign bank, the special servicer of the loan for Fannie Mae.

"The purpose of this letter is to respond to your November 26, 2010 letter, which states that it is a 'Qualified Written Request' pursuant to the Real Estate Settlement Procedures Act (RESPA),

12 U.S.C. Article 2605(e) regarding the loan. However, RESPA is not applicable to the loan because it is not 'secured by a first or subordinate lien on residential real property (including individual units of condominiums and cooperatives) designed principally for the occupancy of from one to four families;' 12 U.S.C. Article 2602 (1) (A). Thus, no response from Fannie Mae or Sovereign Bank is necessary."

Signed by Lawrence P. Rochefort.

The Latell Peppertree Apartment buildings, as well as the Latell Croix Apartment buildings, were designed and built to meet all building codes at the time, as four unit attached buildings, two of which are stand-alone four-unit buildings. I can say this with certainty and authority being that I was a registered Florida engineer who designed the buildings and a licensed Florida general contractor who built the buildings.

By 'misinterpreting' the situation, Lawrence P. Rochefort and Peter C. Triano wrongly denied information required by federal law to be provided to me upon lawful request.

Chapter 5: Stealing Our Properties

The setup was there, unintentional, but it was created by the Federal Housing Finance Agency being the conservator of Fannie Mae.

The FHFA mission was/is to "provide effective supervision, regulation and housing mission oversite of Fannie Mae, Freddie Mac and the Federal Home Loan Banks to promote their safety and soundness, support housing finance and affordable housing and support a stable and liquid mortgage market."

'Words without action' as Fannie Mae was to become a partner in the conspiracy to steal U.S. Government taxpayer bailout money.

The circumstances were a housing market on a steep climb, a Florida market to convert multi-family rental properties to condominiums, a rush to buy multi-family rental properties, properties over-appraised, lenders over-lending and investors over-borrowing.

Fannie Mae and other lending institutions were in serious trouble.

When the housing bubble of 2001 – 2007 burst, it caused a mortgage security meltdown. This contributed to a general credit crisis.

In 2007, Fannie Mae began to experience large losses in their retained portfolios and subprime investments. In 2008, the sheer size of their retained portfolios and mortgage guarantees led the FHFA to conclude that Fannie Mae would soon be insolvent.

Now we have a government to monetarily bailout establishments that cannot fail.

My story shows how our U. S. Government, with elected people, set up Agencies, Bureaus and Departments meant to see that established rules and procedures were followed to protect the taxpayer's money. These organizations are loaded with unelected people who think they are doing their job and push around a lot of paper. They resist getting involved in controversies, therefore, a lack of oversite. Who oversees the overseer?

When there's opportunity to steal multi-millions of dollars, someone will find it. Peter Triano and Lawrence Rochefort found it. Their superiors and Fannie Mae went along with it. Santander National Bank, Akerman Senterfitt, LLC and Fannie Mae were exposed in this crime to steal taxpayer money.

In December 2010, ignoring our many attempts by phone and by mail to meet with the Fannie Mae's loan servicer and our only contact was with Fannie Mae's attorney Rochefort, said attorney formally filed foreclosure proceedings.

My anger continued; in fact, now it was aggravated. I had developed Croix and Peppertree Apartments. We owned them for 20 plus years. We've never missed or been late on a loan payment and always kept the properties in good condition. I have been good to my tenants and when they had a hardship, I worked with them as best that I could.

Although we experienced a vacancy problem due to the 2008 crash of the economy and damages from tenants losing their jobs, abandoning and taking their anger out on the apartments, we made repairs and upgraded the units. Our occupancy rate was increasing and sufficient to cover the loans.

Obviously, something wasn't right. I could not put my finger on it except "government bailout money."

Since the interest rate for loans had greatly fallen, all I was asking for was a decrease in our loans interest rate. Lyle Preest informed me that he was told by Brook Radcliff, Team Manager Collections Department, Sovereign Bank, that the loans had to be 45 days past due (in default) to consider a loan modification. Sucker me fell for it.

Was Fannie Mae even aware of what was going on? Was this a scheme cooked up by Triano and Rochefort? Assuming this was a scheme being applied to Southwest Florida's multi-family rental financial problems, how much crooked bailout money was involved?

They most likely used their scheme on all Santander Bank's Fannie Mae's loans serviced properties. It is estimated that Santander Bank made a profit of $134,088,000 from their portfolio of servicing Fannie Mae's loans in Southwest Florida.

(Fig. 3 Croix Apartments)

Chapter 6: I Need Help

In early February 2011, Preest and Rochefort attended a hearing with a judge to enter an Agreed Order on a 'Motion to Enforce Assignment of Rents,' whereby a property manager would send reports and forward all net cash flow to Akerman Senterfitt. Preest assumed this would satisfy while loan modifications were being worked out.

For some inexplicable reason, the foreclosures continued unabated. Preest questioned Rochefort why the foreclosures needed to continue to be prosecuted since we had just resolved how the rents and lease assignments would work. We'd already agreed to give control to the bank while we worked out a resolution to the loan modifications. Rochefort replied that the continued prosecution of the foreclosure actions was "just part of the process."

***

On February 9, 2011, after Preest had informed me that things were not going well, I hired John Agnew, Esq. of the Henderson, Franklin law firm as my attorney in regards to the foreclosure actions and to help in my efforts for loan modifications. At this time, upon notification that Agnew was my attorney and upon request from Rochefort, Preest was no longer acting on my behalf.

On February 15, 2011, Agnew wrote to Rochefort: "Attached are my client's requests for modifications of the Latell loans. Included in each request is a cover letter from my client to our firm together with the back-up documents my client used in their preparation of the respective proposal (e.g., operating statement, rent roll, etc.). Please review and discuss the proposals with your client, and let me know its position."

On February 17, 2011 the response from Rochefort included the following: "...unfortunately the modifications are not acceptable and we need to move ahead with the litigation..." There was no offer to negotiate and we were never allowed to meet with the bank's loan workout officer.

Agnew's e-mail to Rochefort (February 23, 2011): "If you already know what Fannie Mae/Sovereign would require to reinstate the loans, please let me know."

On Friday, February 25, 2011 Rochefort replied: "...I believe any reinstatement is subject to Sov Bank & FNMA approval and I further believe for them to even consider, a borrower must bring the loans totally current."

***

In Florida, because of the threat of hurricane's, building a residential home is complex. You need to install steel reinforced concrete footers with building codes to withstand 120 mile an hour wind. If I followed the correct process, in 'good faith,' the homeowner received a sturdy home able to withstand the conditions. But if, for example, I skipped steps two and three, their home would end up being destroyed. Hurricane Ian made landfall on Fort Myers Beach with sustained winds of 150 mph. The new builds are still standing; the rest, completely wiped out.

In 'good faith,' I in turn, followed the process and did everything that the Fannie Mae representatives instructed.

And if Fannie Mae had followed their correct process? My wife and I would still have our retirement nest egg.

Chapter 7: Mediation, Not What I Expected

In Webster's II New College Dictionary 'mediation' means: 'an attempt to effect a peaceful settlement or compromise between disputing parties.'

The court ordered mediation was held June 2, 2011. Physically present was the court ordered Mediator, as well as an attorney representing Fannie Mae. Present from another location by phone was Peter Triano, servicer of the loans, and two Fannie Mae employees.

Present representing 'Latell' were myself, Lyle Preest and my attorney, John Agnew. Andrew Bethke, the owner of the company currently managing our properties was available but refused attendance by Triano. Later, I found out that there was a confrontation between Bethke and Triano. But in the meantime, being a court ordered mediation, who was Triano to say who could or could not attend this mediation? Why didn't Agnew, my attorney, have the balls to shut Triano up?

Being fourteen months since the loan payments were stopped, documents were presented showing the combined two Latell properties with an outstanding loan of approximately $2,350,000.00 and a default penalty - 25% interest, prepayment, and attorney fees - in excess of $1,100,000.00.

Preest and I, believing that the mediation was to discuss and hopefully negotiate an interest rate loan modification, presented a plan to do so.

Triano's response was only the offer of a 'friendly foreclosure,' forgiving of the penalty, no negotiating.

At the time, I was involved in another ongoing bank lawsuit as a plaintiff hoping to recapture a $2,000,000.00 investment. I was led to believe that a non-friendly foreclosure would most likely result in a loan deficiency that would take any money I had (I did not have any) or monies I would receive. Also, I thought I currently had non-recourse loans because the previous Fannie Mae loans were non-recourse, a loan secured by property.

I interpreted 'friendly foreclosure' to be the same as a 'deed-in-lieu of foreclosure,' the latter meaning that the loan would be satisfied and foreclosure proceedings halted.

Believing I had no other choice, I verbally agreed to the 'friendly foreclosure.' Nothing was presented in writing at the time and nothing was signed.

In engineering school, we used a combination of science and math to design structures and solve problems. In mediation that day, there was no problem solving, no structured resolution and compromise never entered the equation.

(Fig. 4 Frank Latell)

Chapter 8: A Helpful Letter

Andrew Bethke, owner of the Florida-based Axiom Management Services, Inc., had contracted with me to manage the Croix and Peppertree Apartments.

In today's world, property management must include everything from effective marketing, tenant placement, to maintaining the properties. An intelligent young man in his late 20's, I thought Bethke fit the bill.

Bethke, separate from managing my properties, owned the 32-unit Bonita Apartments in Cape Coral, Lee County, Florida. Unfortunately, his property also suffered financial loss due to vacancies and a forced reduction in rents. Additionally, it so happened that his loan, although not a Fannie Mae loan, was with the Sovereign/ Santander Bank and his servicing officer was Peter Triano.

Bethke had not prior informed me of this namely because it was none of my business. After the occurrence at the mediation, he felt that his experience with Triano could help me.

Shortly after the mediation I received a surprise letter from Bethke.

(Fig. 5 Bethke Letter)

Andrew W. Bethke
President
Axiom Management Services Inc.
PO Box 101669
Cape Coral, FL. 33910

June 13, 2011

Mr. Frank A. Latell
General Partner
Latell Peppertree Apartments Ltd. / Latell Croix Apartments Ltd.
3027 Broadway, Office
Fort Myers, FL. 33901

Mr. Latell,

Because of the financial detriment you now face as the result of the unprofessional, unjustified sanctimonious actions and decisions made by Sovereign Bank employee, Peter Triano, at your June 02, 2011 mediation hearing for your Croix Apartments and Peppertree Apartments, I believe that it is important that I document and share with you the experience that I had with Mr. Triano in 2009 when I approached Sovereign Bank to preempt looming problems with the rental activities at Bonita Apartments, a 32 unit apartment property that I owned in Lee County Florida (the same county that your Croix/Peppertree Apartments are located).

Between 02/20/2009 and 07/08/2009, based on the log that I kept of all communications with Sovereign Bank employees, I communicated by email and phone with five (5) different Sovereign Bank 'loan modification' representatives, each of whom indicated that he was in charge of reviewing my loan to determine if a loan modification was a feasible solution to the short term financial challenges that Bonita Apartments was facing. Each of the first four (4) Sovereign representatives that I made contact and began exploring possible solutions with either quit or were laid off. The fifth person I dealt with was Peter Triano, whom apparently rose through the ranks quickly as his superiors were fired or quit.

During our first communication Mr. Triano requested that I submit historical financial and operating statements as well as multiple loan modification proposals that I felt would solve the problems at Bonita. I immediately complied with his requests, emailing the information to Mr. Triano on 04/22/2009, thinking that he would give my loan modification request a fair review. For the next two (2) months I attempted to contact Mr. Triano to get feedback on the information and proposals that I had submitted to him. I called Mr. Triano at least five (5) times and every time I got his voicemail, leaving him messages that requested he return my call to discuss my loan. He never responded. Finally on 06/29/2009, I called Mr. Triano and he answered. He stated he was on the

(Fig. 5 page 2)

[Recipient Name]
June 9. 2011
Page 2

other line and would call me back within 30 minutes. By the end of the day (6pm) he had not returned my call. When I called him the following morning he exploded with anger stating that he was busy closing two deals that day and that my loan was a low priority compared to the defaulting loans in Tampa and Orlando that he was currently working on. It seemed that Mr. Triano had no interest in reviewing my loan because it was too small ($1.3MM) for him to consider modifying. With each conversation thereafter, Mr. Triano seemed more irritable and less willing to discuss finding a mutually agreeable solution to Bonita's loan. He seemed to be going through motions towards foreclosure, without considering my modification request. At times he offered encouraging information so that he could obtain from me the most updated Bonita operating information. It is possible that he was trying to sell the promissory note prior to foreclosure (numerous investors stopped in to the Bonita on site office to inquire about rental and occupancy rates, operating costs, etc... not information any prospective tenant has ever requested). When I made my final call to Mr. Triano on 07/08/2009, he told me that the loan was sent to foreclosure. I requested that he provide me his reasoning as to why no negotiation had taken place after I had fulfilled all of his requests. He gave no response.

It is my opinion, based on the way that Mr. Triano handled your case and the deceptive manner that he handled mine, that he lacks the experience (age ~31), the etiquette, and the intelligence for managing the negotiations of loans. He is easily frustrated due his lack of understanding of finance, in particular real estate finance (though he pointed out that he has an undergraduate degree in finance). Additionally, it seems that he uses his position to do what is best for his ego, instead of what is best for the party he represents (Fannie Mae, Sovereign Bank/Banco Santander).

Mr. Latell, your case is not the first in Lee County that has been mishandled by Peter Triano (Sovereign Bank). I hope that my experience will help you and Fannie Mae to rectify any wrongdoing you endured at your 06/02/2011 mediation hearing.

Sincerely,

Andrew W. Bethke
President
Axiom Management Services Inc.

I feel it is important to point out that at the time, I was unaware of Bethke's property financial problems.

But the question was - would Bethke's experience with Triano actually help me?

Chapter 9: A "Snow Job"

Two weeks after the mediation, my attorney John Agnew was pre-sented with a 35-plus page document titled "Settlement Agreement." Some of the conditions of this document included:

10b. The Defendant (Latell) shall allow any potential buyer or interested party to have access to the properties, books and records for review and inspection, notifying the lender of interested buyers and offers, keeping the lender fully advised and obtaining lender's consent prior to entering into any contracts regarding the properties, and subject to lender's approval executing a contract(s) for the sale of the properties with the proceeds to be paid to the lender in event of a sale(s) prior to foreclosure.

10d. Defendant shall not bid or conspire with a third party to bid at the foreclosure sales.

13i. The borrower is to continue managing and operating the properties.

16. Each party will be responsible for its own accounting, legal fees and other expenses.

19. The borrower is to manage and operate the properties from the date of this agreement to the appointment of a receiver or release conditions.

19d. Borrower will continue to use rents to pay necessary monthly expenses with other paid to the lender.

30. The parties waive their right to a trial by jury.

By this proposed settlement agreement, the properties' ownership (title) remain in our name until a foreclosure.

I asked myself, why was this not presented as a deed-in-lieu of foreclosure? If the concern was, and should be, to make sure the titles were clear, that could be done by the normal procedure of a title search.

They were Fannie Mae loans and the servicer was willing to waive the deficiency, so why not the deed-in-lieu, and then, in turn, provide a receiver to manage the properties and transfer the title to Fannie Mae or, Santander Bank, the loan servicer, manage and sell the properties?

Why do our properties have to go forward through foreclosure?

The scheme was to get a court judgment in as large an amount as possible. The 35-plus page settlement agreement was to allow the foreclosure to continue, without interference, in order to get a court monetary judgment for the Government taxpayer to bailout Fannie Mae, as authorized by the HERA.

Other properties that were so far underwater may not have recovered the full mortgage amount, but the deed-in-lieu would have prevented the 25% default (interest accumulation), attorneys' fees and other penalties due to dragging out the foreclosure - nearly half the loan amount in 14 months. In this case the bailout, intended to make Fannie Mae whole, was used to make a profit.

Chapter 10: What Being Ignored Feels Like

Upon his review of the proposed settlement agreement, John Agnew responded by letter to the Fannie Mae attorney, Lawrence Rochefort (Fig. 6). Agnew wrote concerning my willingness to pay for incurred expenses, desire to have loans reinstated, reluctant to give up my livelihood, the proposed settlement agreements liability hazard and asking for a revised proposal.

Three days later I received an email from Agnew (Fig. 7) who wrote that Rochefort's response was a firm 'no!' to reinstating loans and 'no' to revising settlement agreement.

Agnew went on to inform me that he fully expects they will attempt to establish a deficiency judgment against me if we do not settle and that a judgment can persist for 20 years. The next day, following a call between Agnew and Rochefort, I told Agnew that I wanted Rochefort's words in writing.

Upon email request from John Agnew to have it in writing, the same day response via email from Rochefort was, "John, your email account of our discussion is largely correct."

Rochefort stated that Fannie Mae would not let me reinstate under any conditions. There was no legitimate reason for Fannie Mae not to permit my offer of reinstatement in that the previous

10 years of Fannie Mae/Latell loans on these same properties and 5 years into these loans were faultless until this intentional default (loans had to be in default to talk to us) on these properties.

Rochefort's statement had a rather rancid odor. It just didn't pass the smell test. For Rochefort, the Fannie Mae attorney, to make a statement like that showed desperation. For my attorney to let it pass showed ignorance. It also showed that Rochefort was a loose cannon with no control by Fannie Mae. Are Triano and Rochefort on their own pulling this scheme? Did they get in too deep? Fannie Mae, Santander Bank and Akerman Senterfitt, knowing or not, are deeply involved.

(Fig. 6 Agnew Letter to Rochefort; July 11, 2011)

Henderson|Franklin
ATTORNEYS AT LAW

171 S Monroe Street • Fort Myers, FL 33901
Post Office Box 280 • Fort Myers, FL 33902
Tel: 239.344.1100 • Fax 239.344.1200 • www.henlaw.com

Bonita Springs • Sanibel

Reply to
John D. Agnew
Direct Fax Number 239.344.1538
Direct Dial Number 239.344.1364
E-Mail: john.agnew@henlaw.com

July 11, 2011

VIA FAX TO 561.653.5333 & E-MAIL TO
LAWRENCE.ROCHEFORT@AKERMAN.COM AND
AND FAX TO 561.659.6313 & E-MAIL NOELLE.PAGE@AKERMAN.COM

Lawrence P. Rochefort, Esq.
Noelle M. Page, Esq.
Akerman Senterfitt
222 Lakeview Avenue
Suite 400
West Palm Beach, Florida 33401-6183

Re: Fannie Mae v. Latell Croix Apartments, Ltd., et al.
Circuit Court, 20th Judicial Circuit, Lee County, Florida
Case No. 10-CA-060339

Fannie Mae v. Latell Peppertree Apartments, Ltd., et al.
Circuit Court, 20th Judicial Circuit, Lee County, Florida
Case No. 10-CA-060342

Dear Mr. Rochefort and Ms. Page:

Mr. Latell, on behalf of Latell Peppertree Apartments, Ltd. ("Latell Peppertree") and Latell Croix Apartments, Ltd. ("Latell Croix"), wishes to reiterate his previously-extended offer of his willingness and continuous want to reinstate the loans to Latell Peppertree and Latell Croix. Specifically, Mr. Latell is willing and desirous to have the loans reinstated for the full principal balances due, and he is willing to roll into the principal all attorneys' fees currently incurred on behalf of Fannie Mae (despite the apparent lack of reasonableness that accompanies fees in excess of $30,000 in relatively uncontested matters) and roll the interest accrued at the regular note rates of 5.22 percent into the principal balance of the loan as well. The only concession requested is that the loans be reinstated without penalty or default rate interest.

As you are aware, Mr. Latell was the developer of these properties and has owned the Peppertree Apartments and Croix Apartments for 21 and 26 years, respectively. During

Henderson, Franklin, Starnes & Holt, P.A.

39

(Fig. 6 page 2)

Lawrence P. Rochefort, Esq.
Noelle M. Page, Esq.
Akerman Senterfitt
July 11, 2011
Page 2

that period of time until April 1, 2010, he was never late on a single payment. The circumstances surrounding the default in April 2010 include drastically fallen occupancy rates and rental rates — mostly to do with the crash of the economy, but also due in part to the deteriorated condition due to tenants losing their jobs and abandoning the apartment unit. Mr. Latell has worked with his property manager for the four years with limited funds to refurbish all the units to a high standard and increase the occupancy rate. As a result of these efforts, occupancy rates for both apartment complexes are now more than sufficient to cover the debts, pursuant to the original terms of the loans.

There is not now, nor has their ever been, apathy demonstrated by Mr. Latell, with respect to the obligations on the loans. Contrary to assertions made by a certain representative of Sovereign Bank, as the servicer of the two loans, Mr. Latell did, indeed, make numerous efforts to contact Sovereign Bank from the month of default until the filing of the lawsuits in these matters. Specifically, enclosed and marked as Exhibit "A" is a document prepared by Lyle Preest, one of Mr. Latell's financial advisers, evidencing regular attempts at communication with Sovereign Bank, from April 2010 through December 2010. Also enclosed are copies of the Qualified Written Requests submitted by Lyle Preest and to which substantive responses were *never* provided (Exhibit "B"), as well as written authorization by Mr. Latell to Sovereign Bank, formally giving Lyle Preest's contact information to Sovereign Bank, for purposes of facilitating a workout (Exhibit "C"). In reality, it was Sovereign Bank who was unresponsive and apathetic about a resolution, not Mr. Latell — Mr. Latell hoped and expected a workout could have and should have been accomplished early and without the need of attorneys for either side or the associated controversy and expense.

As you may be aware, Fannie Mae has a public mission to expand affordable housing and support the housing markets, and self-proclaims **"our job is to help those who house America."** My client is simply requesting that Fannie Mae hold true to its mission statement, and recognize that a *reconcilable* temporary period of hardship came upon a man who, with respect to these and other properties, had for more than twenty (20) years consistently demonstrated himself to be a good developer, a good borrower, a good source of affordable housing, and was diligent in his efforts and timely in his payments.

Admittedly, the referenced hardship resulted in an unfortunate default of the Latell Peppertree and Latell Croix loans, but Fannie Mae should not take advantage of the default to seize Mr. Latell's livelihood. Clearly, that is not in keeping with an entity whose "job is to help those who house America." Instead, Fannie Mae should be willing to give a single reprieve to an individual who otherwise had made no errors in the twenty (20) plus previous years he had done business with Fannie Mae and other lenders, with respect to these properties.

(Fig. 6 page 3)

Lawrence P. Rochefort, Esq.
Noelle M. Page, Esq.
Akerman Senterfitt
July 11, 2011
Page 3

While I hope the offer, above, renders this latter portion of my letter moot, I am in receipt of the proposed settlement documents provided by e-mail on June 17, 2011. In reviewing them with my client, a wide range of concerns were raised. Generally, the settlement documents are written in such a manner that my client is exposed to additional liability, not only during the course of the proposed stipulated foreclosure, but also after the foreclosure is complete. These types of conditions were not envisioned by either my client or I, when we agreed to entertain the potential of a stipulated foreclosure at our June 2, 2011 mediation. Instead, it was our understanding and expectation that the proposal tendered would be simple and more akin to a deed-in-lieu of foreclosure scenario — with little or no continuing liabilities or contingent liabilities for Mr. Latell, and with Fannie Mae benefiting from nominal documentary stamp expense and the assurance of clear title that comes through a foreclosure action.

So, instead of me redlining through more than one-half of your proposed documents, in the event Fannie Mae rejects Mr. Latell's renewed request to reinstate the loans, I am deferring to you to tender a revised proposal in line with the expectations outlined in the previous paragraph. The release of Mr. Latell as an individual obligor pursuant to his general partnership interest in the respective partnerships does not have the value the bank perceives it to have, my client simply does not have sufficient assets worthy of protection, such that it would warrant his willingness to accept anything approaching the scope of what has previously been proposed. In fact, my client has approached me about obtaining bankruptcy counsel, for the purpose of filing petitions on his individual behalf, as well as on behalf of his partnerships. I state this only to attempt to reinforce your understanding of my client's true financial condition and his lack of reason to be willing to negotiate the minefield that is presented in the proposed settlement documents.

I look forward to hearing from you.

Sincerely,

John D. Agnew

JDA/jc

(Fig. 7 Agnew Email Chain; July 14, 2011)

Windows Live Hotmail Print Message

engage this firm to provide formal written advice as to federal or state tax issues, please contact the sender.

-—Original Message-—

From: Frank Latell [mailto:latell@hotmail.com]
Sent: Friday, July 15, 2011 8:20 AM
To: John Agnew; Lyle Preest
Subject: RE: Latell Peppertree and Latell Croix

John,

E-mail Larry that I want it in writing.

I'll be away most of next week available by cell phone.

                    Frank

Subject: Latell Peppertree and Latell Croix
Date: Thu, 14 Jul 2011 15:58:00 -0400
From: John.Agnew@henlaw.com
To: latellf@hotmail.com; lyle.preest@gmail.com; andlstall@citcom.net

Gentlemen,

I just got off the phone with Larry Rochefort. Unfortunately, he stated in no uncertain terms that "Fannie Mae is not going to let him reinstate under any circumstances" and is not authorizing them to revise the proposed settlement documents. Further, he said "there is not a lot of give and take in that [settlement] document." His/the bank's position is that the proposed settlement documents are essentially "form" documents, tailored to each case, and that the bank's willingness to waive $1-1.5 Million in a deficiency is adequate consideration for the assurances sought in the settlement.

They have asked me to get with you to see if you would like for me to make "reasonable" proposed changes to the documents. If not, they will seek to press forward in their case. Unless you are ready to file an individual bankruptcy petition to seek discharge of the liability, I strongly urge you to consider trying to get the settlement documents revised in accordance with something to which you can agree.

Best regards,

John

John Agnew
Attorney at Law
Henderson, Franklin, Starnes & Holt, P.A.
1715 Monroe Street
P.O. Box 280
Fort Myers, FL 33902
Direct Dial: 239.344.1364
Direct Fax: 239.344.1538
John.Agnew@henlaw.com
www.henlaw.com
Visit our Employment Law Blog at www.swflrawsolutions.com

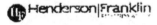 Henderson|Franklin

http://col21w.col121.mail.live.com/mail/PrintMessages.aspx?cpids=274309d2-b208-11e0-96ff-00215a... 8/2/2011

(Fig. 7 page 2)

Windows Live Hotmail Print Message

John, your email account of our discussion is largely correct. I said our client was not interested in reinstatement. I think I referenced that I suspected the total deficiency would be approaching something like a million and that the position of your clients in your latest letter of July 11 didn't make a lot of sense to us in light of the concessions being made. Our client is certainly willing to consider any proposed edits to the settlement documents but it would be counter-productive for you to make wholesale changes to the drafts. Our client relies on representations, warranties and records from borrowers/guarantors and as long as there is open and honest disclosure, most issues can be worked through. Please let us know if how your client wishes to proceed.

On another note, it is time for Sovereign to have an environmental audit done of the property. Para. 13 of its mortgages on the properties addresses this. Can you speak to your client re access for the Bank's consultant? I believe they would like to get out to the property as soon as possible. Thanks, Larry

---

From: John Agnew [mailto:John.Agnew@henlaw.com]
Sent: Monday, July 18, 2011 11:05 AM
To: Rochefort, Lawrence (Sh-WPB)
Subject: FW: Latell Peppertree and Latell Croix

Larry,

Please note the exchange, below. As Mr. Latell requested, I would appreciate it if you would confirm for him (via e-mail or letter through me) that my recitation of Fannie Mae's position is accurate.

Thank you.

John

John Agnew
Attorney at Law
Henderson, Franklin, Starnes & Holt, P.A.
1715 Monroe Street
P.O. Box 280
Fort Myers, FL 33902
Direct Dial: 239.344.1364
Direct Fax: 239.344.1638
John.Agnew@henlaw.com
www.henlaw.com
Visit our Employment Law Blog at www.swflemploymentlawsolutions.com

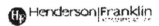

CONFIDENTIALITY STATEMENT

Henderson, Franklin, Starnes & Holt, P.A.

The information contained in this transmission may contain privileged and confidential information. It is intended only for the use of the person(s) named above. If you are not the intended recipient, you are hereby notified that any review, dissemination, distribution or duplication of this communication is strictly prohibited. If you are not the intended recipient, please contact the sender by reply e-mail and destroy all copies of the original message.

To reply to our e-mail administrator directly, please send an e-mail to administrator@henlaw.com

IRS CIRCULAR 230 NOTICE: Pursuant to Treasury Department Circular 230, this is to advise you unless we otherwise expressly state in writing, e-mail communications, including all attachments, from this firm are not intended or written to be used, and cannot be used, for the purpose of avoiding tax-related penalties. If you wish to

http://col121w.col121.mail.live.com/mail/PrintMessages.aspx?cpids=274309d2-b798-11e0-96ff-00215a... 8/2/2011

Chapter 11: My Senses Shouted Fraud!

Upon review of the proposed settlement agreement, the Fannie Mae foreclosure, and attorney Lawrence Rochefort's response, my senses shouted fraud!

According to Preest, Sovereign Bank said that the loans had to be 45 days in default before we could talk modification. Preest had informed me that Lawrence Rochefort said, "Fannie Mae would rather work out a deal to get 100% of the loans repaid versus fore-closure." Yet at mediation, after Preest presented a proposed interest rate modification plan, Triano's response was a flat "take it or leave it," – which was described as a so-called-friendly foreclosure, or coming after me for a $1,100,000+/- deficiency.

On July 24, 2011, I wrote, on behalf of my wife and I, to Rochefort:

We have given considerable thought to the Plaintiff's pro-posed settlement agreement and related attachments. We find it in good conscience that the agreement is unacceptable to us in its entirety and certainly NOT presented in the spirit of mediation we were expecting. We find this documentation prejudicial, overbearing and a downright "bullying" effort by the Sovereign Bank to ramrod us into this egregious agreement that is not even close to being reasonable - only unilateral. Two subsequent proposals we presented demonstrated a 100% repayment of principal and interest to FNMA without losses. Furthermore, 1) the settlement agreement eliminates all rights we may have in discovering why the bank ignored our continued requests for a loan modification beginning over 12 months ago and 2), even eliminates our right to bid on the property at a foreclosure as well as many other "handcuffs."

We outlined our proposal, again, a few weeks ago only to be "snubbed" by the bank, while many other lenders have openly worked with borrowers, who have cash flow properties, to resolve default issues in this economy. The bank's delays in responding have only added administrative and legal costs to this effort.

(Fig. 8 Frank Latell Letter to Rochefort)

Larry,

Mr. Latell has relacted your client's proposed settlement agreement. For his detailed response, please see the message below.

Regards,

John

——Original Message——
From: Frank Latell [mailto:latellf@hotmail.com]
Sent: Sunday, July 24, 2011 4:44 PM
To: John Agnew
Subject: Response to FNMA

We have given considerable thought to the Plaintiff's proposed settlement agreement and related attachments. We find it in good conscience that the agreement is unacceptable to us in its entirety and certainly NOT presented in the spirit of mediation we were expecting. We find this documentation prejudicial, overbearing and a downright "bullying" effort by the Sovereign Bank to ram-rod us into this egregious agreement that is not even close to being reasonable – only unilateral. Two subsequent proposals we presented demonstrated a 100% repayment of principal and interest to FNMA with out losses. Further, 1) the settlement agreement eliminates all rights we may have in discovering why the Bank ignored our continued requests for a loan modification beginning over 12 month ago, and, 2) even eliminates our right to bid on the property at a foreclosure as well as many other "handcuffs".

We outlined our proposal, again, a few weeks ago only to be "snubbed" by the Bank, while many other lenders have openly worked with Borrowers that have cash flow properties, to resolve default issues in this economy. The Bank's delays in responding have only added administrative and legal costs to this effort.

Respectfully Submitted,

Latell Peppertree Apartments, LTD

By: Peppertree Apartments of Lee County, Inc., General Partner

———————————————

By: Frank Latell, President

Latell Croix Apartments, LTD

By: Croix apartments of Lee County, Inc., General Partner

———————————————

p://co121w.col121.mail.live.com/mail/PrintMessages.aspx?cpids=352d8b57-b6f9-11e0-b456-0021...   7/27/2011

Chapter 12: Sneaky Way Out

During the foreclosure proceedings, several requests were made to produce any and all documents governing, relating to or concerning the relationship of Fannie Mae and Sovereign Bank with respect to the Fannie Mae/Latell loans. All requests were met with objections or otherwise ignored.

As a result, our counsel filed a motion in the foreclosure proceedings to compel production of these documents. Fannie Mae's response to the court was to object to these requests on the basis that we were allegedly seeking documents that were "not relevant" and "not reasonably calculated to lead to the discovery of relevant or admissible evidence."

At the court hearing, the Fannie Mae attorney, Lawrence Rochefort, was present by telephone. At first, it appeared that the Judge was going to compel Fannie Mae to produce the documents. Rochefort then argued that I might somehow "misuse" the information provided. Being that Rochefort was available by phone, my attorney was asked to approach the Judge's bench. Since my hearing aids were not the $7,000 variety, I could not completely follow the conversation but I was able to overhear Rochefort's absurd allegation, once again, that I would somehow misuse the information in the documents.

It was ordered and adjudged that Fannie Mae should be required to produce the non-privileged documents if, and only if:

1a. Fannie Mae proceeds with a deficiency proceeding against Latell after the foreclosure sale of the property at issue, or

1b. Fannie Mae does not proceed with the foreclosure sale of the property at issue and instead requests that this Court enter a monetary judgment for which execution could occur against Latell.

2. If Fannie Mae is required to produce said documents pursuant to paragraph 1 above, the documents shall be produced for use solely in this case and subject to attorney's eyes only.

Defendants (Latell) may move this court for relief of "the attorney's eyes only" portion of the Order after receipt of the produced documents if "good cause" could be established.

In other words, Fannie Mae was given the option to hide relevant discovery if it did not seek a deficiency against me. Of course, since Fannie Mae knew it would not suffer any losses regardless - since it was going to be reimbursed for its 'imaginary losses' from the U.S. taxpayer - this was no 'penalty' at all.

Worth noting:

This hearing was recorded by a court reporter. Three years later, I requested a copy of the court recorded hearing, but was informed that they had been destroyed.

Looking back, I see my attorney being very weak in his representation of my case. The judgment from the court "for attorney's eyes only" was demeaning and does not make sense. It is a pre-judgement based on BS from Rochefort.

Chapter 13: Exposing the Fraud

In America today, bullying is getting kicked out the door. But I was being bullied and frustration led me to take action.

I wrote to individuals and organizations that I assumed had the authority and responsibility to protect borrowers from misrepresentations, bullying, fraud and non-compliance with federal law including:

Federal Housing Finance Agency (FHFA)

Federal Bureau of Investigation (FBI)

Office of the Comptroller of the Currency (OCC)

– previously known as Office of Thrift Supervision

FHFA, Office of the Inspector General

Florida Office of Financial Regulations

Governor of Florida Rick Scott

Florida Attorney General Pam Bondi

Consumer Finance Protection Bureau

Florida Congressman Connie Mack

Florida Senator Marco Rubio

Florida Senator Bill Nelson

All with copies to:
CEO Fannie Mae
CEO Sovereign Bank/Santander U.S. Head

Responses included:

"Contact someone else!"

FHFA, Office of the Inspector General wrote that, "they would pass it on to the FHFA."

The Federal Housing Finance Agency (FHFA) indicated that I had reneged on a verbal agreement reached at mediation to accept a friendly foreclosure and that, "our loans have been reviewed by Fannie Mae and Sovereign Bank." I call this "the fox guarding the chickens."

The Consumer Financial Protection Bureau wrote that, "their review was limited to Federal Consumer Financial Protection laws within their authority and that I should contact a private attorney or file my own case in court."

Some did not respond.

In return of my copies sent to Sovereign Bank/Santander U.S. Head, I received four letters, three from Alan D. Wiener, Esq. (no trouble remembering this name with New York Congressman Anthony Weiner making the news), Senior Legal Workout Advisor, and one from Carlos M. Garcia, Chief of Staff of the President and Chief Executive Officer who stated: "The loans are owned by FNMA (Fannie Mae) and Sovereign Bank as the loan servicer can make recommendations to FNMA as to requested loan modifications but the ultimate decision as to whether to modify a loan is made solely by FNMA and Sovereign Bank must act in accordance with the decision by FNMA. According to our records, FNMA has denied your request for modifications of the loans."

Congressmen Connie Mack, Senator Marco Rubio and

Senator Bill Nelson - to their credit - each contacted Fannie Mae and got the same email, forwarded to me, from Carlus K. Flowers, Government and Industry Relations, Fannie Mae.

There was no attempt to resolve the default. The servicer lied to Fannie Mae, who bought it hook, line, and sinker. Fannie Mae stays silent while the servicer commits the fraud.

(Fig. 9 Carlus Flowers Letter; August 12, 2011)

Spielman, Mathew

From:	Congressional Casework
Sent:	Friday, August 12, 2011 12:05 PM
To:	Spielman, Mathew
Subject:	Congressional Inquiry Mack, Connie (Frank Latell) outgoing

Hello Mathew:

This communication is in response to your inquiry on behalf of your constituent, Mr. Frank Latell ("Borrower"), in regard to his interest in multifamily properties known as Latell Peppertree Apartments and Latell Croix Apartments located in Ft. Myers, Florida (the "Properties").

As the Borrower's inquiry discloses, in April 2010, the Borrower defaulted on its payment obligations for the Fannie Mae loans that are secured by the Properties (the "Loans") and the Loans remain in default. Since the payment default, Fannie Mae's servicer for the Loans, Sovereign Bank attempted to resolve the default with the Borrower; however, we understand those attempts by the servicer were unsuccessful.

Due to the default, Fannie Mae commenced formal foreclosure proceedings against the Property in October 2010. In June 2011, the Borrower, Fannie Mae, and the servicer participated in a mediation in an attempt to resolve the default. Through the mediation, an agreement was reached whereby the Borrower would not contest the foreclosure in exchange for releases of certain liabilities of the Borrower. The documents necessary to effect the agreement were prepared and distributed; however, we understand that the Borrower has not executed the documents. Since the Loans remain in default and the Borrower has failed to perform under the mediated agreement, Fannie Mae will continue to pursue its rights and remedies in accordance with the applicable loan documents and local law.

Thanks.

Carlus K. Flowers
Government and Industry Relations
Fannie Mae

This e-mail and its attachments are proprietary, confidential, pre-decisional, not for publication, and contain Nonpublic Information under a Financial Agency Agreement with the U.S. Department of Treasury. If received in error, contact the sender and delete this e-mail and its attachments. Confidential treatment required."

Chapter 14: My Fellow Americans

At the time, I felt a strong obligation to tell Americans that their money was being stolen. But how?

Standing on a soapbox and shouting did not appeal to me. The cost of articles in the newspapers or magazines was out of the question, however, there were many highway billboards all over the country always filled with advertisements or announcements.

I found the cost of a billboard to be reasonable; if I remember correctly, the cost was $500 for three months.

Ocala, Florida is in Marion County situated in the middle of Florida. South and east of Ocala, is Wildwood, which sits nearby a large development named The Villages and near the junction of Interstate 75 and the Florida Turnpike. This intersection is often referred to as the "crossroads of Florida," because traffic can split to Orlando, Miami, Tampa or Naples. Great place to post my warning.

Traffic was fast and my message would be competing with the many other billboards. Keep the message short and to the point, I said to myself.

But…the results were not what I expected; I had one email response.

(Fig. 10 Billboard)

Chapter 15: "Above His Pay Grade."

Sometimes the pen is mightier than the sword.

As a result of a letter sent to the Office of the Comptroller of the Currency and cc'd to Fannie Mae, I received a phone message from the Fannie Mae Resource Center left on my home phone and on my cell phone: "This message is for Frank Latell. This is Fannie Mae's Resource Center responding to a letter you sent. When you get a chance, please call back 1-800-732-6643."

Upon calling the Fannie Mae Resource center, being put on hold and eventually being asked why I was calling, I stated that, "You called me and I am returning your call."

"Oh, that was Ron."

Ron came on the phone and said that the servicer, not Fannie Mae, makes the decisions. During our conversation, I asked to have our conversation in writing.

"No," Ron replied, refusing also to give me his last name and only saying that his employee ID was number 8350B.

Ron said that they (FNMA) "will not modify, or reinstate the loans." This decision, he added, was up to the servicer (Sovereign Bank) and that the "higher-ups" had investigated the situation.

At the end of our conversation, I saved the voicemail

message, then wrote to the OCC, with a copy to Michael Williams, CEO FNMA (Fannie Mae).

The Office of the Comptroller of the Currency was established by the National Currency Act of 1863 and regulates banks and thrift institutions. In fact, their website says, "Ensuring a safe and sound federal banking system for all Americans."

Good. The OCC was also supposed to impose corrective measures when needed.

The CAG, Customer Assistance Group within the OCC, was set up to help customers resolve issues.

In my letter, I recounted my conversation with Ron, including Ron's statement that FNMA would not reinstate my loans and that the situation had been investigated.

To which I had asked, "How could they have investigated since they had not spoken to me nor anyone connected to me?"

No answer.

But the million-dollar question to Ron, and now to the OCC was, "Would FNMA rather foreclose and come after me personally for a $2,000,000 deficiency, which includes the $1,100,000 plus per diem in fees and penalties, than simply reinstate the loan and not suffer loss of principal?"

Ron's response? A hesitant, "Yes."

(Fig. 11 Latell letter to the OCC; October 27, 2011)

Latell Peppertree Apartments, Ltd
Peppertree Apartments of Lee County, Inc., General Partner
Latell Croix Apartments, Ltd
Croix Apartments of Lee County, Inc., General Partner

Frank Latell, President
5422 Peppertree Drive
Ft Myers, FL 33908

October 27, 2011

Comptroller of the Currency (OCC)
Customer Assistance Group (CAG)
1301 McKinney Street, Suite 3450
Houston, Texas 77010-9050

Subject: Case # 01704750/Sovereign Bank

CAG,

For your information, although I have not received a reply of my 2nd letter to the OCC/CAG dated 9/13/2011, here is an update for your file.

On October 19, 2011, The Fannie Mae Research Center left me a message to return its call regarding my letter I sent to the OCC/ CAG with a copy to FNMA. I returned the call, without name or extension, and after some time was connected with someone named "Ron". This is how our discussion went.

Ron said they (FNMA) would not modify, or reinstate the loans. This decision is up to the servicer (Sovereign Bank). He said "higher-ups" had investigated the situation. I inquired then to know how they could have investigated since they have not spoken to me nor to anyone connected with me. He did not answer.

(Fig. 11 page 2)

I requested if, I could appeal the decision. He answered "No", only that I could contact Fannie Mae legal.

I requested for this decision to be sent to me in writing. The answer was "No". I said I should be recording this conversation – again, no response.

I requested Ron's last name. He said they do not give last names, but his employee number is "8350B".

I asked Ron if FNMA would rather foreclose on us and come after me personally for about a $2,000,000 dollar deficiency (this includes the $1,100,000+ per diem in fees and penalties) than simply reinstate the loan and not suffer loss of principle. His response was a hesitant – yes!

One would assume that since I sent my letter to Michael Williams, CEO of FNMA, and that this referenced phone call is a result of that letter, Ron is speaking for Mr. Williams. I doubt it.

Obviously, the copy of my letter to the OCC never reached Mr. Williams and obviously, some underlings made the decision not to reinstate the loans and, obviously, and under – underling. Employee # 8350 B. was assigned to make the call to me to say that "higher-ups" made decisions not to consider my pleas to reinstate my loans on my cash flowing properties.

Obviously, I am very disturbed the way this has been handled by FNMA. I have pointed out the FBI 2010 mortgage fraud report, the Federal Housing Finance Agency findings of "critical supervisory concern" regarding credit losses in their annual examination of FNMA and the Brian Ellis Real Estate letter evidencing FNMA admitting pushing for foreclosures instead of loan modifications.

Sovereign Bank and FNMA tell us the other is responsible for any decisions. Mr. Alan Wiener's (Sovereign Bank) letter of August 26,2011 (copy previously forwarded) states "Requests for modifications of the loans require approval by FNMA, and were rejected by FNMA". As stated in this letter, Mr. Employee # 8350B told me that the decision is up to Sovereign Bank. This is an endless loop of pointing fingers.

(Fig. 11 page 3)

We have cooperated with all involved. I personally made sure the property was improved and properly managed(without compensation) and took the occupancy from 70% to a cash flowing asset of over 90%, during the default stage.

I am dumbfounded by FNMA's attitude of "foreclosure at any cost" concerning our loans and consider FNMA/Sovereign Bank actions as defrauding and criminal.

I am requesting your assistance to urge Sovereign Bank/FNMA, whichever is in charge, to reconsider and meet for modification of the loans.

Thank you for your continuing investigation of my complaint.

Frank Latell, PE, President of the Corporate General Partners

Copies to:
Jorge Moran, President and CEO Sovereign Bank/Santander - US Country Head
John Agnew, Esq. Henderson Franklin Law Firm
Michael Williams, CEO FNMA
Florida Office of Financial Regulations
Edward De Marco, Acting Director, Federal Housing Finance Agency
Federal Bureau of Investigation – Ft Myers Field Office
Congressman Connie Mack, US House of Representatives
Senator Marco Rubio, US Senate

Chapter 16: The Scheme's Working

At the end of each day, my wife and I would hash over "the good, the bad and the ugly" of our day's experiences. The year 2012 brought about the phrase "Foreclosure Sale." Ugly doesn't even come close to how we felt.

The Croix and Peppertree Apartments were sold to qualified buyers via the internet. Santander Bank acted as the loan servicer for Fannie Mae.

Croix Apartments:

A court foreclosure judgment (amount owed Fannie Mae, holder of the mortgage) had been ruled in the amount of $1,203,642.26.

Santander Bank bought the Croix property with the high bid of $400,100.00. Santander Bank had a paper sale (amount a third-party buyer is to pay for the property) agreement for $1,195,000.00. Although Fannie Mae held the mortgage, Fannie Mae and Santander Bank were passed over and the property title was transferred directly to the buyer of the paper sale.

Santander Bank made a profit of $794,900.00 (paper sale high bid $1,195,000.00 minus $400,100.00) with no out-of-pocket monetary investment.

Fannie Mae gets the amount of the high bid of $400,100.00. Due to the taxpayer bailout, Fannie Mae also gets the amount of the difference between the foreclosure court judgment and the foreclosure sale high bid ($1,203,642.26 minus $400,100.00) in the amount of $803,542.26.

Peppertree Apartments:

A court foreclosure judgment had been ruled in the amount of $2,588,263.23.

Santander Bank acquired the Peppertree Apartments with the high bid of $860,100.00 and title bypasses Fannie Mae and was transferred to PBE Companies, LLC, a subsidiary of Sovereign/ Santander Bank.

Three months later, PBE Companies, LLC transfers title to a South American investor for the amount of $2,300,000.

Santander Bank makes a profit of $1,439,900 (sale to investor high bid, $2,300,000.00 minus $860,100.00).

Fannie Mae gets the amount of the high bid of $860,100.00. Due to the taxpayer bailout, Fannie Mae also gets the amount of the difference between the foreclosure court judgment and the foreclosure sale high bid ($2,588,263.23 minus $860,100.00) in the amount of $1,728,163.23.

Through the three appraisals of the Croix Apartments, Santander Bank knew its value and had a buyer prior to the foreclosure sale. Being the mortgage holder, Fannie Mae - through the foreclosure bid process - should have acquired this property and sold it to the buyer, without a taxpayer bailout. The scheme worked allowing the title to go directly to the buyer with profit to Santander Bank. Fannie Mae received the bailout.

Additionally, through the three appraisals of the Peppertree Apartments, Santander Bank knew its value. A sale within three months showed that the title should have gone to Fannie Mae then sold to the buyer, without a taxpayer bailout.

I sent the following letter and 'what happened' and 'follow the money' to every member of the U. S. Congress:

(Fig. 12 Letter to Congress; January 7, 2013)

7 January 2013

Frank Latell
5422 Peppertree Drive
Fort Myers, Florida 33908
E-mail   hasstolen@gmail.com
              (may not respond 2,2,13 thru 2,9,13)

To every US Senate and House of Representatives member

Enclosures: (1) photo of interstate highway billboard
                    (2) WHAT HAPPENED!!!
                    (3) FOLLOW THE MONEY

Gentlemen and Gentlewomen:

It is every elected official's duty to protect the taxpayer's money.

See enclosures.

I've informed several Federal Agencies who ignore, pass the buck, or don't seem to have a problem with it.

What are you going to do about it?

Frank Latell

Copy to:
   President Barack Obama
   Vice President Joe Biden
   The news media

No response.

Chapter 17: The True Story

As discovered later in the Requirements of the "Fannie Mae 2010 Servicing Guide Updates" (Chapter 26), the so called "Settlement Agreement" or "Settlement Documents" referred to in John Agnew's email of 14 July 2011 forwarding Rochefort's email that the "Settlement Agreement Documents" are false, not Fannie Mae documents. They are written to entice the victim by offering a forgiveness of millions of dollars of owner's financial deficiency to let the foreclosure continue without interference.

Get your calculators out.

This was how Peppertree and Croix properties proceeded with the foreclosure and government bailout:

Peppertree Apartments
Foreclosure Judgment $2,588,263.23
Foreclosure Sale $ 860,100.00
Deficiency $1,728,163.23

Croix Apartments

Foreclosure Judgment	$1,203,642.26
Foreclosure Sale	$ 400,100.00
Deficiency	$ 803,542.26

Government taxpayer bailout (Peppertree and Croix) $2,531,705.49

From the Fannie Mae Servicing Guide: "A Deed-in-Lieu of Foreclosure may be accepted if other relief measures or foreclosure prevention alternatives are not feasible." Staying with my story this far, it is obvious that I had the means and the desire to keep the properties. With a Deed-in-Lieu of Foreclosure there would be no 2 years of foreclosure proceedings, excessive Court costs, excessive attorney fees and excessive 25% interest penalties. For the purpose of explaining how the bailout money was stolen, the following is shown how proceeding under a Deed-in-Lieu of Foreclosure would occur:

Peppertree Apartments

Fannie Mae takes title with a mortgage of	$1,589,342.42
Fannie Mae servicer sells property	$2,300,000.00
Fannie Mae profit	$ 710,657.58

Croix Apartments

Fannie Mae takes title with a mortgage of	$ 747,925.63
Fannie Mae servicer sells property	$1,195,000.00
Fannie Mae profit	$ 447,074.37

Fannie Mae profit (Peppertree and Croix) $1,157,731.95 (no bailout)

Santander Bank (having three appraisals for each of the properties and knowing their value) acquired said properties at the foreclosure sale. How Santander Bank profited:

Peppertree Apartments

    Santander Bank buys Peppertree Apartments $ 860,100.00

    Santander Bank sells Peppertree Apartments $2,300,000.00

    Santander Bank profit $1,439,900.00

Croix Apartments

    Santander Bank buys Croix Apartments $ 400,100.00

    Santander Bank sells Croix Apartments $1,195,000.00

    Santander Bank profit $ 794,900.00

Santander Bank profit (Peppertree and Croix)$2,234,800.00

I was wrongly informed by my attorney that "a nonfriendly foreclosure would most likely result in a loan deficiency."

The offer of a forgiveness of the deficiency was a leverage used to keep the foreclosures going, generating more deficiency and a bigger bailout. Rochefort was falsely claiming that Fannie Mae was forgiving the deficiency. With the government bailout to Fannie Mae there was no deficiency.

Final Foreclosure Summary Judgments of the Peppertree Apartments $2,588,263.23 and Croix Apartments $1,203,642.26 did not include attorney fees. They were to be acquired in addition to, as specified. Attorney fees were in excess of $30,000 at the time of mediation and obviously increased during the six months prior to foreclosure. The Foreclosure Summary Judgment for Peppertree Apartments included, "Interest shall continue to accrue from the date hereof on the total sum due Plaintiff of $2,588,263.23 plus attorneys' fees and costs, at the rate of four-and three-quarter percent (4.75) per year from this date through February 29 of this year. Thereafter, the interest rate will adjust in accordance with Section 55.03, Florida Statutes, until the total sum due Plaintiff is paid in full. Plaintiff also is entitled to recover its attorney's fees and costs from defendants, but Plaintiff must establish the amount and reasonableness of said fees and costs." This was also included in the Foreclosure Summary

Judgment for the Croix Apartments.

No attempt was made to recover attorney fees or a deficiency of the Fannie Mae loans.

At this time, I had not discovered the smoking gun (Chapter 26). Triano and Rochefort saw their scheme in jeopardy of being discovered and did not want to aggravate it.

Our properties and your tax money were stolen.

Chapter 18: What Am I Doing?

Without the personal funds needed to pay for the expected attorney fees, I spent a lot of time searching for an attorney or a law firm that would take my case on a contingency fee, payable only in the event of a successful or satisfactory outcome.

I was not getting any takers.

But I thought back to the response I got from the Consumer Financial Protection Bureau: "We hope you understand that the CFPB does not represent individuals in legal matters. Our disposition should not be considered to be a determination with respect to the validity of your complaint. If you believe this does not resolve your complaint, you are, of course, free to contact a private attorney about this matter or file your own case in court."

Knowing that I am a terrible speaker in front of an audience, this appeared very scary. Yet overpowering my fear was the thought that I did not want to find myself on my deathbed wondering, what could I have been thinking - I let those bastards steal our properties and did nothing about it?

Public Speaking Self-Help

Picture them naked.

Went to a Toastmasters meeting; spoke and was awful.

Downloaded Dale Carnegie's Speak More Effectively,
    Part One: Public Speaking A Quick and Easy Way
Got a book from Nolo, 7th Edition;
Represent Yourself in Court, How to Prepare &
    Try a Winning Case
Acquired a list of legal terms
Looked on the internet
Trial tips
How to take a deposition
United States District Court, Middle District of Florida,
    Guide for Proceeding without a Lawyer
Hired a paralegal and consulted with John Agnew

I was ready. Sort-of.

I filed my Complaint in the Circuit Court of the Twentieth Judicial Circuit in and for Lee County, Florida Civil Division on July 2, 2013 as plaintiff, Frank Latell, against the defendants Sovereign Bank and Peter Triano. Defendants then filed on July 30, 2013 to have this case removed to the United States District Court, Middle District of Florida, Fort Myers Division (a Federal court) case number: 2:13-CV-00565-JES-UAM.

During the one full year of representing myself, I had a prepared draft of my opening statement to the jury. A few excerpts of my twenty-minute statement:

Sovereign Bank and Peter Triano not only stole our properties and our retirement, they stole my pride.

I am not an attorney. Even if the attorneys for Sovereign Bank and Peter Triano make a fool of me, which they will try, or if I make a fool of myself here in this courtroom, the facts are the facts.

I hope you, the Jury, will decide guilt on the part of the defendants, repay us for the loss of our properties and reimburse the U.S. Treasury (the taxpayer) $2,531,705.49 for the bailout of Fannie Mae's so called "losses."

***

Along with numerous other motions to the court, the defendant claimed I did not have standing because the loans were not made to me but to entities Latell Croix Apartments, Ltd. and Latell Peppertree Apartments, Ltd. But Frank and Kathleen Latell were the only owners of these required entities.

The court twice ordered stays prior to a decision on my standing. The decision was made to add Kathleen Latell and the two entities (Latell Croix and Latell Peppertree) to the plaintiffs. This action requires, according to Florida state law, that I must have a Florida licensed attorney representing the entities.

Okay, I thought, I'll bite the bullet.

Chapter 19: The Best That I Can Afford

Once again, seeking a law firm or attorney to take my case, I asked John Agnew for recommendations. Of the three names he recommended, I contacted Matthew Toll of Toll Law.

Matthew Toll was a young attorney, in his late thirties, who graduated from Tulane Law School, and was admitted to the Florida Bar in 2004. He was a partner in a mid-sized firm in Cape Coral, Florida prior to opening his own firm, Toll Law, which was primarily devoted to real estate, family law, personal injury, and general civil litigation. From his practice, Attorney Toll was intimately familiar with property owners who had lost real property due to the housing crisis in the local Southwest Florida area. He was well versed on foreclosed properties with Fannie Mae loans.

I could not get Toll to take my case on a contingency basis, but he offered his services at a reasonable price.

On or about December 4, 2014, Toll Law filed with the same Federal Court what was known as the "Third Amended Complaint," which dropped Peter Triano as a defendant. The defense had argued that Peter Triano was covered under the corporate umbrella of Santander National Bank. Also, due to a name change, the defendant was changed to Santander Bank, National Association, a national banking association.

To meet conditions of standing, the plaintiffs then included Frank Latell, Kathleen Latell, Latell Croix Apartments, Ltd., and Latell Peppertree Apartments, Ltd.

Here we go folks!

(Fig. 13 Third Amended Complaint; December 4, 2014)

IN THE DISTRICT COURT OF THE UNITED STATES
MIDDLE DISTRICT OF FLORIDA
FORT MYERS, FLORIDA

FRANK LATELL, KATHLEEN LATELL,
LATELL CROIX APARTMENTS, LTD,
LATELL PEPPERTREE APARTMENTS,
LTD,

   Plaintiffs,

v.   CASE NO.: 2:13-CV-565-FtM-29CM

PETER C. TRIANO and SANTANDER
BANK,

   Defendants.
_____/

THIRD AMENDED COMPLAINT

   Plaintiffs, FRANK LATELL, KATHLEEN LATELL, LATELL CROIX APARTMENTS, LTD and LATELL PEPPERTREE APARTMENTS, LTD (jointly "Plaintiffs") sue Defendant, SANTANDER BANK f/k/a SOVEREIGN BANK, and state as follows:

PARTIES

1. Plaintiff FRANK LATELL is an individual who is a resident of Lee County, Florida.

2. Plaintiff KATHLEEN LATELL is an individual who is a resident of Lee County, Florida.

3. Plaintiff LATRELL CROIX APARTMENTS, LTD ("CROIX") is a limited partnership with its principal place of business in Lee County, and of which FRANK LATELL and KATHLEEN LATELL are general partners, and have

1

(Fig. 13 page 2)

been general partners at all material times relevant to this action.

4. Plaintiff LATRELL PEPPERTREE APARTMENTS, LTD ("PEPPERTREE") is a limited partnership with its principal place of business in Lee County, and of which FRANK LATELL and KATHLEEN LATELL are general partners, and have been general partners at all material times relevant to this action.

5. Defendant, SANTANDER BANK f/k/a SOVEREIGN BANK ("SANTANDER"), is a corporation organized under the laws of the state of Delaware, and regularly transacting business in the State of Florida.

JURISDICTION AND VENUE

6. This Court has subject matter jurisdiction over this action pursuant to 28 U.S.C. §1332, by diversity of citizenship.

7. The amount in controversy exceeds $75,000.00, exclusive of fees and costs.

8. This Court has in personam jurisdiction over Defendant SANTANDER BANK f/k/a SOVEREIGN BANK, as it regularly conducts business operations within the State of Florida, and has therefore submitted itself to the jurisdiction of Courts of this state, pursuant to the Florida Long-Arm Statute, §48.193, Fla. Stat. Furthermore, the tortious conduct of Defendant SANTANDER BANK f/k/a SOVEREIGN BANK alleged herein occurred within the State of Florida.

9. Venue is appropriate in the U.S. District Court of the Middle District of Florida, pursuant to 28 U.S.C. §1391, because Lee County, Florida, is the place where the events alleged herein occurred.

2

(Fig. 13 page 3)

GENERAL ALLEGATIONS

10. Fannie Mae owned and held promissory notes and mortgages taken by PEPPERTREE and CROIX ("the mortgage loans"), which encumbered certain property owned by PEPPERTREE and CROIX known as Croix Apartments of Lee County and Latell Peppertree Apartments of Lee County ("the apartment complexes").

11. SANTANDER was the servicer of the mortgage loans.

12. As general partners of PEPPERTREE and CROIX, FRANK LATELL and KATHLEEN LATELL were jointly and severally liable for the mortgage loans and potential deficiencies thereunder.

13. FRANK LATELL and KATHLEEN LATELL have standing to bring this lawsuit, along with PEPPERTREE AND CROIX, as individuals who have a sufficient stake in the controversy which would be affected by the outcome of the litigation.

14. In or around April, 2010, Plaintiffs sought modifications of the mortgage loans through SANTANDER, due to the housing crisis and economic downturn that was then taking place.

15. On or about April 10, 2010, Plaintiffs, via their agent, Lyle Preest, spoke by telephone to a representative of SANTANDER's defaulted loan department, identified as Brook Radcliffe, and attempted to negotiate a modification of the mortgage loans.

16. Specifically, Plaintiffs sought a reduction in the interest rate on the mortgage

3

(Fig. 13 page 4)

loans.

17. SANTANDER, through its representative, informed Plaintiffs that SANTANDER would modify the mortgage loans if they were in default, but until they were over 45 days past due, SANTANDER would not even consider a modification.

18. Thereafter, in reliance upon SANTANDER's representations concerning loan modification, Plaintiffs purposefully defaulted on the mortgage loans, though they were financially solvent.

19. Once the mortgage loans were in default, Plaintiffs sought modification of the mortgage loans, but their attempts were ignored by SANTANDER.

20. Approximately eight months later, a senior vice President of Santander, identified as Peter C. Triano, advised Plaintiffs to contact the attorney for Fannie Mae.

21. During the period of time that Plaintiffs' modification attempts were ignored by SANTANDER, default interest, at a rate of 25 percent per annum, was accruing on the multi-million-dollar mortgage loans.

22. Upon information and belief, SANTANDER purposefully delayed its response to Plaintiffs, in order to allow the default-rate interest to accrue to such an extent that it would be difficult or impossible for Plaintiffs to reinstate the mortgage loans.

23. Upon information and belief, SANTANDER took this action in order to profit from the subsequent foreclosure sale of the apartment complexes, the market

4

(Fig. 13 page 5)

value of which exceeded the balance owed on the mortgage loans.

24. Further adding to the confusion, SANTANDER misrepresented to Plaintiffs on at least four separate occasions that all decisions to modify are made by Fannie Mae; however, Fannie Mae advised Plaintiffs by telephone on October 19, 2011, from the Fannie Mae Resource Center, that the decision to modify or reinstate is up to the servicer—SANTANDER—and not Fannie Mae.

25. Attached as Composite Exhibit "A" are true and correct copies of several correspondence from SANTANDER to Plaintiffs which claim that modification decisions are made by Fannie Mae.

26. Upon information and belief, SANTANDER purposefully engaged in a systemic deceitful approach to preventing timely decisions to reinstate or to modify the mortgage loans, or to reject proposals for same, in order to create a financial windfall for SANTANDER, in the form of default rate interest.

THE FORECLOSURES

27. Ultimately, foreclosure actions were filed in the Circuit Court of Lee County, Florida, Case Numbers 10-CA-060339 and 10-CA-060342.

28. Mediation was held on June 2, 2011, but despite prior assertions, SANTANDER was completely unwilling to consider a modification under any circumstances.

29. Further, although Plaintiffs offered to reinstate the mortgage loans at the original terms (and forego any prior requests for modification), SANTANDER insisted that reinstatement was not an option, and even a

5

(Fig. 13 page 6)

payoff would require full payment of the default rate interest which had been accruing the date of default, along with pre-payment penalties.

30. At mediation, Plaintiffs reluctantly agreed, in principal, to the only offer made by SANTANDER, which was purported to be a "friendly foreclosure". Instead, the settlement documents tendered by Fannie Mae, via counsel for SANTANDER, exposed FRANK LATELL and KATHLEEN LATELL to additional and extended liability, and such documents were rejected.

31. By the actions of SANTANDER, Fannie Mae was able to obtain final judgments in foreclosures on the apartment complexes, and then to assign the final judgments in foreclosure to SANTANDER prior to the foreclosure sales.

32. SANTANDER thereafter made assignments of its interests in the actions, with SANTANDER's assignees receiving title to the properties after successful credit bids at the sales, with the CROIX apartment complex at a high bid of $400,100.00, and the PEPPERTREE apartment complex at a high bid of $860,100.00.

33. SANTANDER then profited from the sale of the loan or property to a third party, as it is believed to have received the rights and interest to the judgments on the mortgage loans at less than fair market value, then sold them shortly thereafter at substantial profits.

34. The CROIX apartment complex was sold to a third party for $1,195,000.00.

35. The PEPPERTREE apartment complex was sold to a third party for $2,300,000.00.

6

81

(Fig. 13 page 7)

36. Each sale price was well in excess of the principal balance of the respective mortgage loan.

37. All conditions precedent to the filing of this action have been satisfied or waived.

COUNT I – FRAUDULENT MISREPRESENTATION

38. Plaintiffs re-assert the allegations in paragraphs 1 through 37 above.

39. This is an action for fraudulent misrepresentation against SANTANDER.

40. SANTANDER made false statements of fact, inter alia, that Plaintiffs would receive loan modification only after they defaulted on the mortgage loans. Such statement was made by a representative of SANTANDER, identified as Brook Radcliffe, by telephone, on or about April 10, 2010.

41. SANTENDER knew that these statements were false, as it had no intention of granting a loan modification.

42. SANTANDER knew that these statements would induce Plaintiff to act on them, as they were allegedly the steps necessary to achieve the Plaintiffs' goal of loan modification.

43. Plaintiffs did act on the false statements to their detriment, to wit, Plaintiffs intentionally defaulted on the mortgage loans believing that it would make them eligible for modification of the mortgage loans.

44. As a result of their detrimental reliance, Plaintiffs lost their investment in the apartment complexes, and additionally have been alleged to be liable for a seven-figure deficiency on the mortgage loans, while upon information and

(Fig. 13 Page 8)

belief, SANTANDER has profited.

WHEREFORE, Plaintiffs pray that this Honorable Court enter Judgment in their favor, against Defendant, for compensatory damages in an amount consistent with the evidence, together with punitive damages, the cost of litigation, interest, reasonable attorneys' fees, and such other and further relief as the Court deems appropriate under the circumstances.

COUNT II – FRAUD IN THE INDUCEMENT

45. Plaintiffs re-assert the allegations in paragraphs 1 through 36 above.

46. This is an action for fraud in the inducement against SANTANDER.

47. SANTANDER made false statements of fact, inter alia, that Plaintiffs would receive loan modification only after they defaulted on the mortgage loans. Such statement was made by a representative of SANTANDER, identified as Brook Radcliffe, by telephone, on or about April 10, 2010.

48. SANTENDER knew that these statements were false, as it had no intention of granting a loan modification.

49. SANTANDER knew that these statements would induce Plaintiff to act on them, as they were allegedly the steps necessary to achieve the Plaintiffs' goal of loan modification.

50. Plaintiffs justifiably acted on the false statements, to their detriment, to wit, Plaintiffs intentionally defaulted on the mortgage loans in order to obtain loan modification.

51. As a result of their detrimental reliance on SANTANDER's false statements,

8

(Fig. 13 Page 9)

Plaintiffs lost their investment in the apartment complexes and additionally have been alleged to be liable for a seven-figure deficiency on the mortgage loans, while upon information and belief, SANTANDER has profited.

WHEREFORE, Plaintiffs pray that this Honorable Court enter Judgment in their favor, against Defendant, for compensatory damages in an amount consistent with the evidence, together with punitive damages, the cost of litigation, interest, reasonable attorneys' fees, and such other and further relief as the Court deems appropriate under the circumstances.

DEMAND FOR JURY TRIAL AND PRAYER FOR RELIEF

Plaintiffs FRANK LATELL and KATHLEEN LATELL respectfully demand trial by jury, pursuant to Federal Rule of Civil Procedure 38, and pray for judgment against Defendant SANTANDER as follows:

a. Directing Defendant SANTANDER to pay Plaintiffs FRANK LATELL and KATHLEEN LATELL compensatory damages in an amount to be proven at trial;

b. Directing Defendant SANTANDER to pay Plaintiffs FRANK LATELL and KATHLEEN LATELL punitive damages in an amount to be determined at trial;

c. Directing Defendant SANTANDER to pay Plaintiffs FRANK LATELL and KATHLEEN LATELL the cost of litigation of this matter;

d. Directing Defendant SANTANDER to pay Plaintiffs FRANK LATELL and KATHLEEN LATELL reasonable attorneys' fees; and,

e. Granting such other and further legal and equitable relief as this Honorable Court deems proper.

9

(Fig. 13 Page 10)

CERTIFICATE OF SERVICE

I HEREBY CERTIFY that a true and correct copy of the foregoing was furnished via electronic notification through the CM/ECF system to all counsel of record on this ___4th___ day of December, 2014.

/s/ *Matthew S. Toll*

MATTHEW S. TOLL, ESQ.
Florida Bar No.: 0785741
STEPHEN N. McGUIRE II, ESQ.
Florida Bar No.: 0102755
TOLL LAW
Attorneys for **FRANK LATELL,
KATHLEEN, LATELL CROIX
APARTMENTS, LTD, and LATELL
PEPPERTREE APARTMENTS, LTD**
1217 Cape Coral Parkway E., #121
Cape Coral, Florida 33904
(239) 257-1743 (telephone)
(239) 257-1794 (facsimile)
matt@matthewtoll.com
stephen@matthewtoll.com

Chapter 20: How I Got the Best from My Deposition

"If you tell the truth, you don't have to remember anything." I agree with Mark Twain and because of his wisdom, I had no fear of giving my deposition.

Noelle Pankey, the attorney for the defendant, having received no new useful information from me in the first deposition, acquired our personal checking and equity line information from our bank and now took a second deposition of me. Questions and answers of this deposition revealed the exact monthly amounts of the Croix loan payment ($5,099) and the Peppertree loan payment ($10,793) for eight consecutive months from April through November, 2010, were being deposited into our personal checking account. The deposition goes on to show that these funds were used to pay down our equity line on our home and would be readily available for when the dispute was settled.

The purpose of the defendant's attorney was to show that I did not have the funds to make good my offer as put forward by John Agnew, my foreclosure attorney, to reinstate the loans.

The deposition continued showing in excess of $110,000 +/- income (deposit that the defendant's attorney had overlooked) at this time from the U.S. Government (Treasury) and the State of

North Carolina for overpayment of 2006 income taxes.

I believed that the only reason to have this deposition was to trap me. But I had the proverbial last laugh. My having the funds surprised the defendant's attorney to the point where she showed her visible disappointment. She was wrong, did not do her homework and was embarrassed.

My response to her displeasure was that, "I took the money from the government. I got more money from the State of North Carolina as a tax refund. I got money from withholding the mortgage payments. I used most of it to pay down the equity line. I used it for attorney fees and I also put some in a vault."

Of the two depositions, with this same attorney, the first lasting several hours, and this one well into its second hour, she chose this time to say, and I quote, "I asked you to please – to please be good on your agreement at the beginning of this deposition to not speak over me and to let me finish my question before you begin answering."

I apologized.

(Fig. 14 Frank Latell Deposition)

Page 54

1   A. Most likely I did, yeah. I don't know.

2   Q. But you agree that the amount of the April, May,

3 and June 2010 Croix and Peppertree mortgage payments would

4 have been enough to make a $35,000 equity line of credit

5 pay down, correct?

6   A. I do agree to that. Yes, it would have been

7 enough.

8   Q. And if you'll flip to the next page in Composite

9 Exhibit 19, Bates labeled Edison 0169 at the bottom

10 right-hand corner. Are you on that page?

11   A. Yes.

12   Q. If you look at the entry on July 29, 2010, it

13 says that the principal payment and also says that it's

14 for $30,000. Where did the funds for that principal

15 payment come from?

16   A. I don't know at this time.

17   Q. Could they have been from the mortgage payments

18 for Latell Croix and Latell Peppertree?

19   A. Partially they could have been.

20   Q. In July of 2010, did you make principal payments

21 pay down with funds other than those from the mortgage

22 payments?

23   A. To answer your question honestly, let's go back

24 to your Exhibit 18, date 8/10/10.

25   MR. TOLL: It's only page 1 of the statement.

Page 55

1 It's only page 1 of the statement.

2   THE WITNESS: This was on the Edison National

3 Bank statement.

4 BY MS. PANKEY:

5   Q. Yes. And I believe that that's only the first

6 page of the statement, which does not include any checks

7 that were written out of the account.

8   A. No. I'm going back to 8/10/10.

9   Q. Information on the statement?

10   A. The statement dated 8/10/10.

11   Q. The information on the statement dated 8/10/10?

12   A. Yes.

13   Q. Exhibit 18 helped you to answer where the $30,000

14 principal payment dated 7/29/10 on the equity line of

15 credit came from?

16   A. If you look down on 8/10/10, and you look at the

17 deposit for 7/12, there's a deposit of $93,542.

18   Q. Yes. Does that explain the $30,000 paydown to

19 the equity line of credit on July 29, 2010?

20   A. I think it explains some of it possibly. I'm

21 just trying to make these numbers work like you're asking

22 me.

23   Q. Do you know what that $93,542 deposit was from?

24   A. Yes. I exactly know where it's from.

25   Q. What is it?

Page 56

1   A. It was a rebate from the U.S. government on my

2 '06 taxes.

3   Q. It was a tax refund?

4   A. Yes, it was.

5   Q. Did you use the proceeds form your tax refund to

6 pay down your equity line of credit?

7   A. I used it for part of that, I used it for

8 attorney's fees, and I put some of it away.

9   Q. How much of the $93,000 tax return did you use to

10 pay down your equity line of credit?

11   A. I don't know. Whatever these numbers come out

12 to. It was part of what was — what I was holding back

13 from my mortgage payments and this and other things. So I

14 put it at different places, including paying down my

15 equity line. Some of it went to attorney's fees.

16   Q. Of the eight months of mortgage payments that you

17 deposited into your personal checking account, how much of

18 that money was used to pay down your equity line of

19 credit?

20   A. I don't know. You can look at the equity line

21 and see how much it decreased.

22   Q. Did you use the funds from the withheld mortgage

23 payment for anything other than paying down your equity

24 line of credit?

25   A. Yeah, I think I put some of it away.

Page 57

1   Q. What do you mean when you say "I put some of it

2 away"?

3   A. I had a safety account — not account. I had a

4 safety — I kept cash.

5   Q. So you took some of the withheld mortgage

6 payments, the funds, and withdrew it in cash?

7   A. That's correct.

8   Q. What did you do with the cash?

9   A. I put it in a safety deposit box. Well, let's

10 say — let's say a safety vault.

11   Q. Was that at a bank?

12   A. No.

13   Q. Where was that?

14   MR. TOLL: I'm going to object.

15   THE WITNESS: I don't think I got to say where it

16 is.

17 BY MS. PANKEY:

18   Q. But you took out — of the withheld mortgage

19 payment you —

20   A. I took the money from the government. I got more

21 money for the state of North Carolina as a tax refund. I

22 got money from withholding the mortgage payments. I used

23 most of it to pay down the equity line. I used it for

24 attorney's fees and I also put some in a vault.

25   Q. I appreciate that, Mr. Latell, because you did

15 (Pages 54 - 57)

(Fig. 14 page 2)

Page 58

1 actually answer the question that I was going to ask. But
2 like I said at the beginning of this deposition, I asked
3 you, and you agreed, that we would not speak over each
4 other and we'd let each other finish our questions and our
5 answers respectively. If I could please ask you to do
6 that for me going forward, that would be great. Is that
7 okay?
8   A. I'm not quite sure what you just told me.
9   Q. I asked you to please -- to please be good on
10 your agreement at the beginning of this deposition to not
11 speak over me and to let me finish my question before you
12 begin answering.
13   A. All right. If I did that, I'm sorry.
14   Q. Thank you.
15   If I could have you look at Composite Exhibit 19,
16 it's the next page is Bates labeled Edison 0168 at the
17 bottom right-hand corner.
18   A. Yes.
19   Q. There's an entry on 8/17/10 with a principal
20 payment of $19,799.01. Where did the funds from this
21 principal payment come from?
22   A. Part of what we just discussed.
23   Q. Which is what?
24   A. Part of it was from the tax return from the state
25 of North Carolina and from U.S. government. Part of it

Page 59

1 was from the withheld mortgage payments. I think there's
2 more than enough there to cover this 19,000.
3   Q. If I can have you switch to the next page of
4 Composite Exhibit 19, Bates labeled Edison 0157 in the
5 bottom right-hand corner.
6   A. Yes.
7   Q. There's an 8/29/11 entry for home equity check
8 number 114 for $10,000. What was this check for?
9   A. I don't recall at this time.
10   Q. If I could have you flip to the next page, which
11 is the last page, Edison 0155.
12   A. I got it.
13   Q. In the middle of that statement there are three
14 home equity checks listed in varying amounts, 4,000 and
15 change, 1,000 and change, and 6,000. Do you know what
16 those checks were used for?
17   A. I don't recall at this time.
18   Q. Testimony is that while you don't remember the
19 exact dates or amounts, you did use the withheld mortgage
20 payments from the Latell Croix and Latell Peppertree
21 mortgages to pay down this equity line of credit; is that
22 correct?
23   A. Yes, that is correct.
24   Q. When was the last time you spoke with Mr. Proest?
25   A. Year and a half ago, I'm guessing.

Page 60

1   Q. Are you planning to call him as a witness in this
2 case?
3   A. You informed me that he's dead.
4   Q. Yes, I informed you of that. Have you spoken to
5 him?
6   A. I think Steven, the attorney, told me that you
7 told him --
8   MR. TOLL: Hold on. Hold on. I'm going to
9 object to any conversations between you and your
10 lawyer.
11   THE WITNESS: Okay.
12 BY MS. PANKEY:
13   Q. And I'm not interested in what you spoke to your
14 lawyer about. I just want to know if you found out from
15 your lawyer that I informed him Mr. Proest is dead. Have
16 you talked to him since that day?
17   MR. TOLL: You can answer that.
18   THE WITNESS: No. In fact, I've been trying to
19 reach him and that's when I was informed that he was
20 dead.
21 BY MS. PANKEY:
22   Q. When's the last time you tried to reach him?
23   A. Year ago, eight months ago. Actually less than
24 that. Probably six months ago.
25   Q. How did you kind of communicate with him at that

Page 61

1 time?
2   A. E-mail, phone call.
3   Q. Both?
4   A. Yes.
5   Q. And there was no response?
6   A. No response.
7   MS. PANKEY: I believe that that's all the
8 questions I have. But I'm going to take a break for
9 five minutes to go through my notes and make sure
10 that's the case, and then we can finish up.
11   MR. TOLL: Okay. Sounds good.
12   MS. PANKEY: All right. I'll let you all know
13 when I'm back in the room.
14   MR. TOLL: All right.
15   (A brief recess was had.)
16 BY MS. PANKEY:
17   Q. Mr. Latell, I have just a couple more questions
18 and then we'll be done here today.
19   If I could have you get back out Exhibit 15,
20 please.
21   A. I have it.
22   Q. Okay. And you previously testified that the
23 handwritten notes on this document are your handwriting;
24 is that right?
25   A. Yes.

16 (Pages 58 - 61)

I should not have apologized. Pankey was covering for her own screw up. The deposition shortly ended.

Chapter 21: Difficulty of Deposition's

The subpoenas for Fannie Mae employees were refused by Fannie Mae attorneys for reasons that attorneys are famous for…no depositions! Apparently, federal employees do not have to comply with subpoenas if the government does not believe that the private litigation is "important enough" to warrant the time of the employees in question.

Matt Toll informed me of the progress, or lack thereof, in getting Fannie Mae depositions. "Pursuant to your request," he said, "the purpose of this correspondence is to memorialize the difficulties this office has encountered in attempting to produce Fannie Mae representatives to appear for depositions in the above-captioned matter."

This was also the situation when trying to have a Federal Housing Finance Agency employee produced.

We wanted - no needed - those depositions.

Remember at the mediation, there were two, deadly but silent, Fannie Mae representatives present by telephone with Peter Triano at a different location.

Additionally, the attempt to have a deposition from the Akerman Senterfitt/Fannie Mae foreclosure attorney, Lawrence

Rochefort, was denied because he was now defending Santander Bank.

Chickens, fox, and now outfoxed.

Chapter 22: The Lying "SOB"

August 13 - December 7, 2015.

I can testify to the fact that the wheels of justice certainly turn slow, verging on going in reverse.

In August, Matt Toll and I went to the New York City offices of Akerman, (formerly Akerman Senterfitt), for the deposition of Peter Triano. But you wouldn't want to be holding your breath for any progress because it was December before we even received the typed transcript.

To set the stage, you may recall that the Qualified Workout Requests presented by Lyle Preest included letters from Latell Croix Apartments of Lee County, Inc., General Partner and Latell Peppertree Apartments of Lee County, Inc., General Partner to the Henderson, Franklin Law firm dated February 10, 2011. Modifications to the Latell loans were presented to Lawrence Rochefort (copy to Noelle [Page] Pankey) by email of February 15. Rochefort's return email of February 17, stated that the modifications were not acceptable and the need to move ahead with litigation. There was no offer to discuss or negotiate and only an offer of a "friendly foreclosure."

Highlights from the deposition include:

Triano: The offered modification request, with a reduction in interest rates from 5.22% to 2.0%, was unacceptable by the bank, "and by the bank, that would be me (Peter Triano), the workout officer."

Fact: I received (from Sovereign/Santander US Head) three letters from Alan D. Wiener, Esq. Senior Legal Workout Advisor, and one from Carlos M. Garcia, Chief of Staff of the President and Chief Executive Officer that stated, "The loans are owned by FNMA (Fannie Mae) and Sovereign Bank as the loan servicer can make recommendations to FNMA as to requested loan modifications but the ultimate decision as to whether to modify a loan is made solely by FNMA and Sovereign Bank must act in accordance with the decision by FNMA."

Fact: There was no offer to discuss or negotiate and Triano's statement is in total conflict with his seniors at Sovereign/Santander Bank.

Fact: My October 19, 2011 conversation with Ron of the Fannie May Resource Center stated that the decision to modify or reinstate the Latell loans was up to the servicer, Sovereign Bank.

Fact: Finger pointing.

Question to Triano: "A modification or some other arrangement is actually possible all the way through the foreclosure process up until, I guess when, a foreclosure sale?"

Triano: "I guess once before a judgment is issued."

Fact: The letter from John Agnew to have the loans reinstated at no loss to Fannie Mae with a response from the Fannie Mae foreclosure attorney: "Fannie Mae will not let him reinstate under any circumstances."

Triano: "The Latell loans (properties) were a loss to Santander (Sovereign) Bank."

Fact: How could it be a loss? Santander/Sovereign Bank did not own the loans. Four letters from Santander state this.

Question: "Okay. Do you - - but can you testify with any degree of certainty that it was a loss as opposed to a profit?"

Triano: "It was a loss."

Question: "So your formal testimony is the bank lost money on these properties, it gained nothing by virtue of doing a foreclosure?"

Triano: "It gained nothing."

***

Triano: "...we tried for many months to reach Mr. Latell..."

Fact: I am a businessman, my name, address and phone number are publicly listed. Triano also knew, by official correspondence, his means of contact was through Lyle Preest. Preest, once finding out who to talk to, tried contacting Triano and a Sovereign Bank employee referred him to Fannie Mae's attorney, Lawrence Rochefort.

Triano: "...until I had gone down myself without an appointment, just went on my own to see if there was anybody in the leasing office or someone I can try to contact."

Fact: Peter Triano states that he, on a number of occasions, went down there to visit the apartments without having an appointment. WOW! The office was maintained at normal working hours and beyond. I have been assured by Andrew Bethke, owner of the management company, that Triano never came to the properties.

Triano: No analysis was done on the Latell properties and the reason why reinstatement was rejected, "I believe the value of those assets (Latell properties) had declined significantly along with many assets in that southwest region."

Fact: John Agnew's (Latell attorney for foreclosure) letter of July 11, 2011, nine months before foreclosure, states that Mr. Latell has worked with his property manager for 4 years, with limited funds, to refurbish all the units to a high standard and increase the occupancy rate. As a result of these efforts, occupancy rates for both apartment complexes are now more than sufficient to cover the debt, pursuant to the original terms of the loans.

The Latell Croix Apartments were paper sold prior to foreclosure bidding for considerably more than the Latell loan. The Latell Peppertree Apartments were sold three months after foreclosure for considerably more than the Latell loan. Documentation of the sale stated that the Peppertree development was 90% occupied at the time of the sale with well-maintained units and considered a "B" asset (one step below "A," a top-rated asset).

(Fig. 15 Peppertree photo)

(Fig. 16 Peppertree sale; October 2012)

HOME TRENDS OPINION ENTREPRENEURS STRATEGIES COMPANIES INDUSTRIES GOVERNMENT LEGAL NOTICES

TOP DEALS

South American investor buys Peppertree Apartments

BY: SEAN ROTH / REAL ESTATE EDITOR

September 28, 2012

"The bank wound up making a profit," Kattan says. "It was in good shape for a bank-owned deal. It was an older community, but with nice well-maintained units. It was probably a B asset in a C or C+ location."

The Latell Croix and Latell Peppertree Apartments were designed and built as four (4) family attached buildings separated by fire walls. In accordance with the Real Estate Settlement Procedure Act, Section 2605(e), Preest sent two Qualified Written Requests on July 14, and November 26, 2010 to Peter Triano requesting entitled information.

Triano: "Now, we did end up talking to Lyle Preest. But Lyle was, you know, we had stopped communications and we started receiving communications that were going over here. So, it was no longer a - what's the word - amicable situation. It was more of a litigious situation."

Question: "And if you received something, you know, labeled Qualified Written Request, does that in any way disqualify the borrower from a modification or reinstatement because they've made the matter more litigious or -"

Triano: "Um, I would say it depends. I mean, I think in this particular case we tried for many months to reach Mr. Latell, could not speak to him, had to speak to Mr. Preest who could not give much information other than, you know, demands for a modification that were not of, you know, someone that we would take serious."

Fact: Triano LIED. Neither Preest nor I ever talked to him.

Triano: "Every loan is a loan that we originate."

Fact: Mortgages of the Latell Croix Apartments and the Latell Peppertree Apartments were originated by Independence Community Bank and owned by Fannie Mae before Sovereign Bank acquired the servicing of the loans.

Question: "Were you provided access?"

Triano: "Not during the time of appraisal. I don't think at all during the entire process."

Fact: Peter Triano was being untruthful again. On 12/15/2010 an inspection was performed on the mortgage #7207395 (Peppertree Apartments) requiring repairs by Sovereign Bank. Defendants Notice of Serving Expert's Report, filed 8/20/15, refers to six appraisals of which three were performed under Triano's watch (Croix Apartments 9/30/2010 and 7/21/2011, Peppertree Apartments 7/25/2011).

The following is a portion of Peter Triano's sworn deposition taken from the court reporters 120-page transcript.

(Fig. 17 Triano's Transcript)

```
1                    PETER TRIANO

2     with Mr. Latell, after months of trying to

3     reach him.  And then the -- I believe the

4     value of those assets had declined

5     significantly along with many assets in

6     that southwest region.

7                    So we believed with the fact

8     that we were not able to make contact with

9     the borrower, any information we did

10    receive was, I think, showing at the time

11    insufficient income to cover the expenses,

12    let alone the debt that any modification

13    wouldn't really be of any benefit to us.

14         Q.    Well, I'm focusing more on

15    reinstatement as opposed to modification

16    right now.  Let's talk about the months of

17    trying to reach Mr. Latell.  Do you recall

18    what efforts were made to reach Mr. Latell?

19         A.    Yeah.  I know the collections

20    department had made numerous phone calls.

21    And then once the loan was transferred to

22    me, which I believe was sometime -- some

23    point in April or May, that I had tried

24    reaching out after, say, June -- by June,

25    July, tried contacting Mr. Latell, was
```

(Fig. 17 page 2)

1   PETER TRIANO

2   not -- did not receive any call.

3   We generally contact them right

4   away to get their take on what's going on,

5   get the information that we need to look at

6   the property's performance to order an

7   appraisal, because what we want is we want

8   an appraiser to go in there and have access

9   to the units, have access to the income and

10   expenses so that we can get a proper value

11   on it.

12   Otherwise, we have to order it

13   just based on, you know, their opinion of

14   what's going on in the market. Umm, so we

15   tried contacting him and we did that up

16   into, you know, I believe, late that summer

17   until I had gone down myself without an

18   appointment, just went on my own to see if

19   there was anybody in the leasing office or

20   someone I can try to contact.

21   Now, we did end up talking to

22   Lyle Priest. But Lyle was, you know, we

23   had stopped communications and we started

24   receiving communications that were going

25   over here. So it was no longer a -- what's

(Fig. 17 page 3)

```
 1                    PETER TRIANO
 2    the word -- amicable situation.  It was
 3    more of a litigious situation.  So we would
 4    try to go down there and see the property
 5    ourselves without having an appointment.
 6    So I did that on a number of occasions.
 7         Q.    Okay.  Two questions just on
 8    that.  Your records or your file when you
 9    were in the workout group, would that
10    reflect the attempts of communication with
11    Mr. Latell?  Would there be some sort of
12    summary of phone calls or e-mails or
13    whatever mechanisms you would have used
14    with them to communicate with the borrower?
15         A.    No specific call logs.  There
16    may be, if I had an e-mail address, there
17    may be e-mails of attempted communications.
18              But internally on our
19    internally prepared reports that we would
20    do quarterly to senior management, we would
21    have to say what actions were taken, and on
22    there we probably noted that multiple
23    attempts were made to contact the sponsor
24    with, you know, no success.  So that may be
25    potentially out there.
```

(Fig. 17 page 4)

```
1                    PETER TRIANO

2          Q.    And if you received something,

3    you know, labeled qualified written

4    request, does that in any way disqualify

5    the borrower from a modification or

6    reinstatement because they've made the

7    matter more litigious or --

8          A.    Umm, I would say it depends.  I

9    mean, I think in this particular case we

10   tried for many months to reach Mr. Latell,

11   could not speak to him, had to speak to

12   Mr. Priest who could not give much

13   information other than, you know, demands

14   for a modification that were not of, you

15   know, someone that we would take serious.

16              And then these request for

17   documents challenging our -- the fact that

18   we owned the mortgage, I believe, I think

19   there was communications.  So it became a

20   hostile environment from -- after months of

21   trying to communicate.  We had this hostile

22   environment and I think that, you know,

23   made it a tougher situation.

24         Q.    Okay.  This Exhibit 6, I

25   believe there's some discussion about
```

Chapter 23: Judgment Day

Believe it or not, the Judgment and Preest have a connection.

My last contact with Lyle Preest was on June 16, 2014, when he sent me an email providing a new email address and cell phone number alongside his well wishes.

The attorney for the defendant wanted to take Preest's deposition. Their search unearthed Lyle Preest's death certificate dated October 23, 2014.

Preest's death certificate stated that he died in the Suncoast Hospice Care Center Mid-Pinellas Park, Florida, but I felt that if he was ill, he would have contacted me. I called the Hospice Care Center as to the nature of his illness and how he died; understandably, they would not give me any information without the consent of family. Under the circumstances of my trial, Preest's untimely death raises suspicion of foul play.

***

Highlights from the Opinion and Order of the Federal Court of March 22, 2016:

Page 3:

"The Court has already determined that Frank and Kathleen have standing and that each suffered a distinct injury that gives them standing to bring the instant action. Plaintiffs further respond that Santander Bank cannot prove it did not make the misrepresentation, and there are genuine issues of material fact still in dispute which prevent Summary Judgment."

Page 5:

"Fannie Mae owned and held promissory notes and mortgages (the "loans") of Peppertree Ltd. and Croix Ltd., which were secured by apartment complexes owned by Croix Ltd. and Peppertree Ltd. The loans were serviced by Santander Bank, who also owned and held the notes and mortgages at times."

Note: Santander (Sovereign Bank) acquired the servicing only of the mortgages from Independence Bank, which had ultimately failed. The notes and mortgages were owned by Fannie Mae and serviced by Independence Bank. Santander Bank never owned the notes or mortgages.

Page 10:

"Frank may have liability for a deficiency amount, and therefore Frank has standing to pursue his claim in this case."

Page 11:

"Frank has constitutional standing."

Page 12:

"That portion of defendant's motion seeking summary judgment for lack of standing is denied."

Page 15:

"The alleged communication at issue was made to Mr. Preest, who is now deceased. Mr. Preest's deposition was not taken, so the issue is whether his version of the conversation, as he told it to others, is somehow admissible. Because it is not, and there is no admissible evidence of the existence of any misrepresentation, summary judgment is due to be granted in favor of the defendant."

Page 18:

"The only reason Frank did not make the mortgage payments was in reliance on the misrepresentation that the loans had to be forty-five (45) days past due before a modification could be considered. This is sufficient evidence of reliance as to non-payment of the then-late April payment and the subsequent monthly obligations. Reliance is at least a disputed issue of material fact, and therefore summary judgment is inappropriate on this ground."

Page 19:

"The evidence in this record (regarding Santander's Motion for Summary Judgment based on Promise of Future Action as a Basis of Fraud) is sufficient to at least create a material issue of disputed fact, and therefore the motion is denied on this issue."

The essence of this Opinion and Order resulting in an order to the Clerk of Court to terminate any pending motions, enter judgment accordingly, and close this case, is that the Plaintiff's key witness has deceased making his evidence hearsay and therefore inadmissible.

***

I think some higher power meant for me to write this book.

Chapter 24: Imagining Retribution

Fatto un torto. Peter Triano, the Fannie Mae loan servicer and the Fannie Mae foreclosure attorney, Lawrence Rochefort, have all done me wrong and thinking back to my Italian heritage, I imagined taking revenge.

My dad was a very good father and resident of our small town in Girard, Ohio. He also happened to be very knowledgeable of what was going on at that time. And although he was this straight-forward and upright citizen, he had connections to the shady side of the Italian community.

We lived on Ella St., in an old house that was originally my mother's father's house and was up the hill from the railroad. A block from us on Stambaugh St. was a house converted into a grocery store. One day my father and I walked down to the store, the second house from the corner, and then up the steps. Inside, I noticed that the store owner was physically impaired with a bad leg. As an impressionable five-year-old, I remember well that he had a terrible time getting around.

"What's wrong with his leg?" I innocently asked my dad

while walking home.

"Apparently," my dad replied, "the guy got on the wrong side of 'certain' people who decided to teach him a lesson - he was shot in the knee."

Now, back to present day. I recently went to the town of Girard for a funeral. I had the occasion to see the site of the store. Not much has changed except the side road got paved and the old house is still there. And not much has changed when I think of Triano.

Being that I thought murder would not go well with God, I imagined a good old-fashioned knee capping was in order, just like the ones the IRA dished out on a regular basis during the height of the so-called Troubles in Northern Ireland circa 1970-80s. I'm half-ashamed to admit that I wanted gunshots in each of Triano's knees and one elbow would be suitable. I thought that leaving one good arm would be justified, in that it would not be fair for someone else to have to wipe his stronzo!

(Fig. 18 The old store.)

Chapter 25: Tony

My late father, Tony Latell, was an Italian immigrant, who came alone to America at the age of 17. Like most immigrants, he struggled, earning a few extra bucks making and selling wine at $2.00 per gallon during the days of prohibition.

He was a good father and head of the family. Once there was a bitter argument between my mom and dad; afterwards I distinctly remember Dad saying to me and my brothers, "always side with your mother!"

Dad worked in the town tannery, when that closed, he worked in the nearby steel mill. He was always thinking of a way to make extra income. One summer we had a fruit and frozen custard stand. At Christmas time we sold Christmas trees. Dad rented an empty lot on the main road down from home and my Uncle Frank, an electrician, wired the lot for beautiful night lighting. One year, the last week before Christmas, we were low on trees. Dad said, "Go buy out the two or three other lots selling trees in Girard and get them at a low price." Made our place the only lot in town with trees. Smart man.

Tony had injured his back in an industrial accident, which required him to wear a brace. One crowded Sunday morning at

Mass, he was not wearing his brace. Feeling faint, he went out to the front entry, sat on a low rail, passed out and fell 6 feet. He broke his neck.

He was only 52. Fortunately, his expenses were covered by the Ohio Industrial Commission. Dad lived for another 25 years residing in Northside Hospital, Youngstown, Ohio. After the initial shock and recovery, Tony accepted being a quadriplegic. Although lacking in schooled education, he was an intelligent and outgoing person. Everyone knew Tony. Having a motorized wheelchair and able to get around, he was an inspiration to many who came in feeling sorry for themselves. In the hospital, Tony started a television rental business. This made him more money than he knew what to do with.

For me, after my return to civilian life, my father's money helped get me started as a designer, builder and developer. And now what does Tony have to do with my case?

For four years, my team and I tried to get the Fannie Mae loans service agreement by:

A. Request, during foreclosure, by John Agnew to Fannie Mae attorney, Lawrence Rochefort. Refused.

B. When requested by John Agnew, acting as Frank Latell's foreclosure attorney in Civil Court, the Court granted it only if Fannie Mae came after Frank Latell for a deficiency.

C. Requested by Frank Latell when acting as self-representation. Refused.

D. Requested by John Agnew when acting as Frank Latell's (Plaintiff) attorney. Refused.

E. Requested by Matthew Toll when acting as Latell's attorney. Refused.

F. Peter Triano's deposition, when asked about Fannie Mae guidelines, 56/4-15, "There is a live platform that Fannie Mae has as their guidelines. It's a very long owner's document that is a continually updated live document. So, it's not like you can print, you know, print out chap -- you know, version, you know, for 2005 and, you know, that was what you had. It's a live document, continuously evolving." A nervous and evasive answer and will prove to be one of many lies.

G. On February 23, 2016, I (Plaintiff) filed with the Court to compel the third request for production from Santander (Defendant) copies of any servicing agreement between the Santander/Sovereign Bank and Fannie Mae related to the servicing of the loans at issue in this matter. Santander Bank argued that the documents requested are protected from disclosure based on the work product privilege.

***

Now, back to my dad. Since my father's passing, I have been surprised and blessed to have him, who I believe is my angel, wake me up at night, remind me of stuff and tell me to get up and go write it down because, "Frank my boy, you'll never remember it in the morning!"

Anyway, it's okay if you don't believe in angels, but I do.

In the meantime, curiosity got the best of me and I went on the internet for information on angels.

Are angels and humans alike?

No, angels do not marry or reproduce like humans. (Calm down, Dad.)

What is the job description of angels?

We don't know whether every angel carries out the same tasks or whether some of them specialize in certain areas.

This last answer really got my attention, because as my 'Angel, Chief of Staff,' one day in 2016, Tony downright forced me to stay at my computer and type in: Fannie Mae service guide.

115

The first thing up: Fannie Mae 2010 Servicing Guide Update Part VII and Part VIII. The guide was dated April, 2010 - the exact month and year I stopped payments!

Peter Triano, loan servicing officer of Santander Bank, and Lawrence Rochefort, Fannie Mae foreclosure attorney, knew what the Fannie Mae guide required and made every effort to keep this guide from me and my attorneys and the Fannie Mae servicer never did get us a copy of the loan service agreement.

(Fig. 19 Tony)

Chapter 26: The Smoking Gun

I have found the smoking gun! And although disappointed that it was so close after the Summary Judgment, I still felt elated.

The Fannie Mae 2010 Servicing Guide Update Part VII and Part VIII was 361 pages and there were several pertinent sections that dealt directly with our loans.

Preface Page iii: Part VII discussed servicing functions that pertain to the management of delinquent mortgages or mortgages where the likelihood of default is reasonably foreseeable, and Part VIII addressed foreclosure procedural requirements. (Requirements being the key word here regarding my properties.)

"Although servicers are encouraged to implement the new requirements as soon as possible, they have a mandatory effective date of January 1, 2011...Servicer's must use diligent efforts to implement them as soon as feasible, but in no event later than January 1, 2011."

Page V: "The servicer must make sure that its staff is thoroughly familiar with the contents and requirements of the servicing guide as it now exists and as it may be changed from time to time."

Part VII, Chapter 4, Section 403.01 Payment Reduction Plan

(11/01/09): "The payment reduction plan (PRP) provides a borrower with temporary payment relief while the servicer and the borrower work together to find the appropriate permanent foreclosure prevention solution."

Part VII, Chapter 6, Section 602 Mortgage Modifications (01/01/09): "A servicer must consider modification of a mortgage loan that is delinquent or for which default is reasonably foreseeable (imminent) under circumstances similar to the following: A borrower who has experienced a permanent or long-term reduction in income is unable to continue making the mortgage payments."

Part VIII, Chapter 1, Section 203, Reinstatements (01/31/03): "The servicer can accept a full reinstatement of a first mortgage loan even if foreclosure proceedings have already begun."

Lawrence Rochefort quoted to my foreclosure attorney, John Agnew, "Fannie Mae will not let him reinstate under any circumstances." Rochefort later verified this in writing. Being Fannie Mae's foreclosure attorney, he was knowledgeable of the requirements of the servicing guide. Now I know why Rochefort kept me and my attorney from getting it during the foreclosure proceedings.

Santander Bank's Fannie Mae loan servicing officer lied at the deposition regarding the Fannie Mae servicing guide. Peter Triano was fully aware of the servicing guide as stated that the servicer's staff must be thoroughly familiar with its contents and requirements. There was no doubt that Rochefort and Triano both lied regarding this document.

On review of the Fannie Mae 2010 Servicing Guide Update, Part VII (Delinquency Management and Default Prevention) and Part VIII (Foreclosures, Conveyances and Claims, and Acquired Properties), I find no mention of a "Friendly Foreclosure," which was the only offer (no negotiations) from the Fannie Mae loans servicer (Santander/Sovereign Bank, loan workout officer, Triano) at the Court ordered mediation of June 2, 2011. The "Friendly Foreclosure" (forgiveness of delinquency) was the only offer in lieu of a pursued $1,100,000+ delinquency.

An email from Agnew on July 14, 2011 stated that Rochefort told him, regarding the friendly foreclosure, "There is not a lot of give and take in the settlement documents." The bank's (loan servicer) position was that the proposed settlement documents are essentially "form" documents.

The 35-plus page friendly foreclosure settlement document was not a Fannie Mae document or any other recognized foreclosure document and was in fact created by Rochefort for the Latell properties and possibly other Fannie Mae foreclosed properties (John Agnew email of 7/15/2011 quoting Rochefort, "documents are essentially form documents tailored to each case.")

This document was created to allow the foreclosure to proceed. Fannie Mae, Rochefort and Triano wanted the foreclosure to proceed and to be lengthy (25 percent default penalty) to provide a large court monetary judgment.

The court monetary judgment is used to "prove" a "loss" to Fannie Mae and to allow Fannie Mae to be reimbursed by the bailout provided by the Housing Economic and Recovery Act of 2008 (HERA).

During my foreclosure mediation, the Fannie Mae personnel in silent attendance sanctioned the "Friendly Foreclosure."

Chapter 27: Between a Rock and a Hard Place

The crux of this story was the acquisition of the Fannie Mae 2010 Servicing Guide Update Part VII and Part VIII. Fannie Mae has put themselves between a rock and a hard place.

1. Lawrence Rochefort, Fannie Mae's foreclosure attorney, said to Lyle Preest, Latell's representative, he was sure FNMA would rather work out a deal to get 100% of the loans repaid versus foreclosure (from Preest's reporting in writing to me).

2. The foreclosure mediation of June 2, 2011 involved a Fannie Mae foreclosure attorney who was physically present. Peter Triano, the Fannie Mae loan servicing officer, attended via phone from an undisclosed location. With Triano were the 2 Fannie Mae employees who obviously were knowledgeable of the loans in question and the servicing guide, or they would not have been part of this mediation. Their silence throughout the mediation tells a story in itself.

3. The Fannie Mae Resource Center phone call to me asking to return the call; the return call conversation stating that the servicer makes the decisions, the refusal to put it in writing, and the refusal to give his full name all come into questioning.

4. Fannie Mae did not dispute my accounting of the telephone conversation put into my letter of October 27, 2011 to the Office of the Comptroller of the Currency (OCC) with a copy sent to Michael Williams, CEO FNMA (Fannie Mae) and others (telling of the phone conversation since Fannie Mae would not put it in writing).

5. Carlus K. Flowers, Government and Industry Relations, Fannie Mae, responded with five letters, two to Congressman Connie Mack, two to Senator Mark Rubio, and one to Senator Bill Nelson that Fannie Mae inquired through the servicer, Sovereign Bank, and that the attempts to resolve the default were unsuccessful. Contrary and to the fact, the servicer's loan officer, Peter Triano, ignored attempts by the borrower (me). Fannie Mae never consulted the borrower (me) in its inquiry of this matter.

6. The FHFA is the conservator of Fannie Mae. As a result of my letter to them, the Federal Housing Finance Agency (FHFA) responded by letter of December 30, 2011. "Your loans have been reviewed by the Fannie Mae Resource Center, Congressional Inquiries Office, the multifamily business and the servicer Sovereign Bank. Your request for a loan modification was denied. The denial was provided to you in writing by both the servicer and Fannie Mae's Congressional Inquiries Office." This is incorrect - my telephone conversation with the Fannie Mae Resource Center indicated that the decision to modify or reinstate the loans was up to the servicer. Fannie Mae, when asked, said they would not put it in writing.

7. The Service Workout Action Template (SWAT) is a form required and prepared by the Fannie Mae loan servicing agent and sent to Fannie Mae periodically regarding the recommended strategy for foreclosing and/or enforcing defaulted loans. In October, 2010, the servicer submitted a SWAT alleging that the borrower was non-responsive. The servicer recommended commencing

foreclosure. At that time, Lyle Preest was trying to make contact with the loan servicing officer. We did not even know who it was. Fannie Mae has no checks on its servicer.

8. Fannie Mae and its conservator, Federal Housing Finance Agency, refused the subpoena for employees involved in this case to appear for deposition.

The Fannie Mae 2010 Servicing Guide Update Part VII and Part VIII was obviously, and painstakingly, put together to guide the Fannie Mae loan servicer. It answers nearly every question and when a question arises, the guide instructs one where to call. Its obvious intent was to help the servicer and to help those with troubled loans.

Fannie Mae stock is sold on Wall Street. Fannie Mae is in the business of making money for the company. Therefore, one can only believe that the employees of Fannie Mae are pressured to make money. Their loyalty obviously was to Fannie Mae, ignoring their own servicing guide and allowing, even requiring, the servicer to harm the borrower if doing so maximized profits.

Through the Housing Economic and Recovery Act of 2008 (HERA), the U.S. Government opened the door to let the thieves come in.

A meeting was held with me, a retired lawyer friend, my son, Matthew Toll, and his associate. The Fannie Mae Servicing Guide Update Part VII and Part VIII was the main focus of that meeting - was the guide just a guide or did it have teeth regarding its requirements? As a result of our discussion, Matt Toll sent the following certified letter to Fannie Mae dated June 21, 2016 (Fig. 19).

As of this printing, Fannie Mae has not responded to Toll's letter, which was sent to the Washington, D.C. main office with copies to 5 Fannie Mae regional offices.

Maybe some fancy lawyer explanation will try to weave between the explicit requirements of the guide and the fact that this guide was ignored by the servicer and that Fannie Mae knowingly let it happen. Fannie Mae is between a rock and a hard place.

Santander National Bank is implicated in this conspiracy through its employee, Peter Triano, for his intentional failure to work with me, the borrower, his efforts to avoid and hide the servicing guide and its requirements, and his lies under oath.

Ackerman LLP is implicated in this conspiracy through its employee and shareholder, Lawrence Rochefort (the Fannie Mae foreclosure attorney) for his intentional failure to work with me or my attorney, his efforts to avoid and hide the Fannie Mae Servicing Guide and its requirements, and to lie in his quote to John Agnew, my foreclosure attorney, "Fannie Mae will not let him reinstate under any circumstances."

By staying silent, Fannie Mae is complicit in the act of stealing our properties.

(Fig. 20 Matt Toll Letter; June 21, 2016)

TOLL LAW

Matthew S. Toll, Esq.
Nadine Goodman, Esq. +
Tammy Page, Esq. +

Attorneys at Law
1217 Cape Coral Parkway East #121
Cape Coral, Florida 33904
www.capecoralfamilyattorney.com

Telephone: (239) 257-1743
Facsimile: (239) 257-1794

+Of Counsel

June 21, 2016

Federal National Mortgage Association
"FANNIE MAE"
3900 Wisconsin Avenue, NW
Washington, DC 20016-2892

*Via Certified and Regular U.S. Mail
and Facsimile (202) 752-3868*

Re: FANNIE MAE 2010 SERVICING GUIDE UPDATE PART VII and PART VIII
Our File No: 14/94

To Whom it May Concern at FANNIE MAE:

Please be advised that this office represents the interests of a number of property owners (both residential and commercial) who have outstanding mortgages owned by FANNIE MAE. As you know, these mortgages are often serviced by 3rd parties (typically banks, credit unions, or other financial institutions). As a foreclosure defense attorney, my goal is often to help the property owner "save" their property, typically through some type of loan modification or reinstatement of a loan that is in default (or that is allegedly in default).

One of the primary difficulties that I face in my practice is to determine exactly who has authority "to make a deal." Often times, the attorneys for the servicer allege that FANNIE MAE is the ultimate decision-maker. However, representatives from the FANNIE MAE resource center often allege that the servicer is the ultimate decision maker. While this merry-go-round circles, properties that could be saved are being foreclosed, and losses are being realized that are not necessary.

To determine the truth to this matter, I have uncovered what appears to be detailed instructions as to how FANNIE MAE owned mortgage loans are supposed to be serviced. Enclosed herewith, please find a copy of the FANNIE MAE 2010 SERVICING GUIDE UPDATE PART VII and PART VIII. In reviewing same, it appears that servicers which are servicing FANNIE MAE loans are REQUIRED to comply with same. Please advise as to the following:

1) Are the requirements set forth in the FANNIE MAE 2010 SERVICING GUIDE UPDATE PART VII and PART VIII formal requirements or merely guidelines?

2) Is there a similar guide for commercial properties? If so, can you provide this office with a copy? We will pay the postage and copying costs.

3) Does the servicer have a legal duty to comply with the servicing guide?

4) What are the consequences of a servicer's failure to comply with the servicing guide?

127

(Fig. 20 page 2)

5)   Can you provide my office with the other parts of the servicing guide along with the most recent version? We will pay the postage and copying costs.

6)   Is there a form servicing agreement between FANNIE MAE and its servicers? If so, can you provide this office with a copy? We will pay the postage and copying costs.

A written response would be appreciated. If you have any questions, comments, or concerns, please do not hesitate to contact this office.

Sincerely,

Matthew Toll, Esquire
Enclosures
cc: Client
FANNIE MAE Northeastern Regional Office, 1835 Market Street, Suite 2300, Philadelphia, PA 19103-2909
FANNIE MAE Southwestern Regional Office, International Plaza II, 14221 Dallas Parkway, Suite 1000, Dallas, TX 75254-2916
FANNIE MAE Southeastern Regional Office, 1075 Peachtree Street NE, Suite 1600, Atlanta, GA 30309
FANNIE MAE Western Regional Office, 135 North Los Robles Ave., Suite 400, Pasadena, CA 91101-1707
FANNIE MAE Midwestern Regional Office, One South Wacker Drive, Suite 1400, Chicago, IL 60606-4667

(Fig. 21 Preface Fannie Mae Servicing Guide)

Fannie Mae
2010 Servicing Guide Update
Part VII and Part VIII

April 2010

(Fig. 21 page 2)

April 28, 2010

Preface

This *Servicing Guide Update* consists of *Part VII, Delinquency Management and Default Prevention,* and *Part VIII, Foreclosures, Conveyances and Claims, and Acquired Properties. Part VII* discusses servicing functions that pertain to the management of delinquent mortgages or mortgages where the likelihood of default is reasonably foreseeable, and *Part VIII* addresses foreclosure procedural requirements and the servicer's general administrative and property management functions for acquired properties.

This update includes the incorporation of previously issued announcements that have impacted *Parts VII* and *VIII.* In addition, Fannie Mae is adding or updating a number of new policies and procedures. Refer to SVC-2010-06 for details about all of the changes that have been incorporated.

Servicers should follow the instructions in this *Preface* when using the updated 2010 *Parts VII* and *VIII* in conjunction with the 2006 *Servicing Guide.*

Effective Dates for the 2010 *Servicing Guide Parts VII* **and** *VIII*

The effective date for each section is the date that is shown in parenthesis next to each section title. If multiple changes with different effective dates were made to the same section, only the most recent effective date is shown. Generally, although servicers are encouraged to implement the new requirements as soon as possible, they have a mandatory effective date of January 1, 2011.

However, the new requirements regarding Servicing Standards and Collection Procedures (*Part VII, Chapters 1* and *2*) are particularly important and material to Fannie Mae's ongoing efforts to keep borrowers in their homes and to reduce credit losses. Accordingly, servicers must use diligent efforts to implement them as soon as feasible, but in no event later than January 1, 2011. Further, Fannie Mae may direct servicers on an individual basis to implement some or all of the new Servicing Standards and Collection Procedures for all or particular segments of their Fannie Mae portfolios by a specific date in 2010 as Fannie Mae determines to be necessary or appropriate. In the event Fannie Mae directs servicers to

(Fig. 21 page 3)

Preface

Using the 2006 Version of
the Servicing Guide with the
Updated Parts VII and VIII

April 28, 2010

implement the new Servicing Standards and Collection Procedures by a specific date in 2010, servicers must take any additional steps necessary to comply.

Using the 2006 Version of the *Servicing Guide* with the Updated *Parts VII* and *VIII*

For the sections in *Parts VII* and *VIII* that are now effective (effective on or before April 28, 2010), servicers must use the updated *Parts*. For the new or updated policies that are not effective until January 1, 2011, servicers must follow the previous requirements as described in *Part VII* and *VIII* of the 2006 version of the C rte er(as amended by Amnnr nee me no , r until either the earlier of the date implemented by the servicer or the mandatory effective date. In addition, servicers must continue to follow *Parts I – VI, IX – XII* of the 2006 version of the *Servicing Guide* (as amended by *Announcements*).

For ease of use, when viewing the 2006 version of *Parts VII* and *VIII* in AllRegs, servicers will see a link to the 2010 version of the *Part.*

Note: The Table of Contents for *Parts VII* and *VIII* in the 2006 *Servicing Guide* reflects the 2006 version of those *Parts*. Refer to the new Table of Contents for the new organization of the updated a e np rc EHand d Fa rln addition, links from the 2006 version to b enerd l nnd d Rwill take the user to the 2006 version of the *Part.*

Access Options

Fannie Mae currently offers the 2005 and 2006 versions of its c eo iei f r *Guide*, related *Announcements* and *Lender Letters*, and the updated *Parts VII* and *VIII* through a variety of mediums, including:

- using a free electronic version on the AllRegs Web site through a link from eFannieMae.com;

- a subscription paid directly to AllRegs for an enhanced electronic version with additional features and a higher degree of functionality (than the free version); and

(Fig 21 page 4)

- a subscription to Fannie Mae through eFannieMae.com for printed copies of the *Servicing Guide* and all servicing-related *Announcements* and *Lender Letters* that are distributed through postal mail.

The updated *Parts VII* and *Part VIII* are also available in PDF format on eFannieMae.com.

Amendments to the *Guide*

Fannie Mae may at any time alter or waive any of the requirements of its *Servicing Guide*, impose other additional requirements, or rescind or amend any and all material set forth in its *Servicing Guide*. The servicer must make sure that its staff is thoroughly familiar with the content and requirements of the *Servicing Guide* as it now exists and as it may be changed from time to time.

Notification of Changes and *Guide Updates*

Fannie Mae notifies servicers of changes and updates to its *Servicing Guide* policies and procedures -- as communicated in *Announcements, Lender Letters*, and Notices -- in two ways:

- by posting the documents on eFannieMae.com and the AllRegs Web sites,

- by e-mail notification of those postings to servicers that subscribe to Fannie Mae's e-mail notification service and select the option "Servicing Policy Updates."

Forms, Exhibits, and Content Incorporated by Reference

Information about the specific forms that servicers must use in fulfilling the requirements contained in the *Servicing Guide* is provided in context within the *Guide*. Servicers can access the actual forms in several ways:

- on eFannieMae.com via the Single Family Forms and Documents page, which provides a complete list of forms as interactive PDF files;

(Fig. 21 page 5)

- on the AllRegs Web site via embedded links in the free electronic version of the *Servicing Guide* (and through a searchable database with a full subscription to AllRegs Online).

Some materials are only referenced in the *Servicing Guide* and are posted in their entirety on eFannieMae.com. In addition, from time to time, Fannie Mae issues specific guidance, which is incorporated into its *Servicing Guide* by reference. Such specific information -- whether it currently exists or is subsequently created -- and the exhibits referenced in the *Guide* now or later are legally a part of this *Servicing Guide*.

Technical Issues

In the event of technical difficulties or system failures with eFannieMae.com, with the delivery of the "Servicing Policy Updates" option of Fannie Mae's e-mail notification service, or with the AllRegs Web site, users may contact the following resources:

- For eFannieMae.com and Fannie Mae's e-mail notification service, use the "Contact Us" or "Legal" links on the Web site to ask questions or obtain more information.

- For the AllRegs Web site, submit an e-mail support request from the Web site or contact AllRegs Customer Service at (800) 848-4904.

When Questions Arise

Servicers that have questions should contact their Servicing Consultant, Portfolio Manager, or the National Servicing Organization's Servicer Support Center at 1-888-FANNIE5 (888-326-6435) unless specifically instructed otherwise within this *Guide*.

Chapter 28: Aiding, Abetting and Conspiracy

Lawrence Rochefort of Akerman and Peter Triano of Santander National Bank hid the guide from us and intentionally lied about the guide; at this point, through my attorney, I petitioned the Florida Circuit Court with my complaint of aiding, abetting and conspiracy.

Lawyers for the Defendants threatened sanctions against myself and my attorney, Matthew Toll. Given the size of this case and the personal risks involved, Toll was forced to withdraw from representing the Plaintiffs in this action. In accordance with Florida law, I dropped the other Plaintiffs from the case and while a non-lawyer cannot represent an entity, I can legally represent myself.

At this point, in November of 2016, my only remaining choice was to represent myself and pursue the relief set forth in my First Amended Complaint.

(Fig. 22 First Amended Complaint; November 2016)

IN THE CIRCUIT COURT OF THE TWENTIETH JUDICIAL CIRCUIT IN AND FOR
LEE COUNTY, FLORIDA   CIVIL ACTION

FRANK LATELL, KATHLEEN LATELL,
LATELL CROIX APARTMENTS, LTD, a
Florida Limited Partnership, and LATELL
PEPPERTREE APARTMENTS, LTD, a
Florida Limited Partnership,

     Plaintiffs,

v.   CASE NO.: 16-CA-003460

AKERMAN LLP, a Florida Limited Liability
Partnership, LAWRENCE ROCHEFORT,
individually, and PETER TRIANO,
individually,

     Defendants.

_____/

FIRST AMENDED COMPLAINT

Plaintiff, FRANK LATELL sues Defendants, AKERMAN LLP, a Florida Limited

Liability Partnership, LAWRENCE ROCHEFORT, individually, and PETER TRIANO,

individually, and in support thereof, states as follows:

PARTIES

1.   Plaintiff, FRANK LATELL, is a resident of Lee County, Florida who is

      otherwise *sui juris*.

2.   Defendant, AKERMAN LLP, is a Florida Limited Liability Partnership

      doing business in Lee County, Florida.

3.   Defendant, LAWRENCE ROCHEFORT, is a licensed Florida attorney

      based of Palm Beach County, Florida. LAWRENCE ROCHEFORT has

      subjected himself to the jurisdiction of this Court due to his dealings with

1

(Fig. 22 page 2)

Plaintiff in Lee County, Florida as described in this Complaint. At all material times relevant to this complaint, LAWRENCE ROCHEFORT was employed by AKERMAN LLP (formerly known as AKERMAN SENTERFITT LLP) and acted within the course and scope of his employment. AKERMAN LLP is responsible for the actions of LAWRENCE ROCHEFORT as described herein under the legal doctrine of *respondeat superior*.

4. Defendant, PETER TRIANO, is a resident of New York. PETER TRIANO has subjected himself to the jurisdiction of this Court due to his dealings with Plaintiff in Lee County, Florida as described in this Complaint.

5. This Court has *in personam* jurisdiction over Defendant PETER TRIANO, as he regularly conducts business within the State of Florida, and has therefore submitted himself to the jurisdiction of Courts of this state, pursuant to the Florida Long-Arm Statute, *§48.193, Fla. Stat.* Furthermore, the tortious conduct of Defendant, PETER TRIANO, alleged herein occurred within the State of Florida.

6. Plaintiff demands a jury trial on all issues so triable.

7. The Plaintiff was previously involved in a lawsuit against SANTANDER BANK, N.A. (although the original suit was against SOVEREIGN BANK, the predecessor-in-interest to SANTANDER BANK, N.A.). The lawsuit in question accused SANTANDER BANK, N.A. of fraud.

2

(Fig. 22 page 3)

a. The lawsuit was originally filed in the 20th Judicial Circuit in and for Lee County, Florida (case number 13-CA-1806).

b. The lawsuit was removed to federal court on July 29, 2013. The federal case number was 2:13-CV-565-FtM-29CM (Middle District of Florida, Fort Myers division).

c. Despite a number of motions to dismiss, the Plaintiff was ultimately able to overcome same, and conduct discovery. During the course of the federal litigation, SANTANDER BANK, N.A. took a number of actions to prevent full and complete disclosure in response to the Plaintiff's discovery requests.

d. The federal case was ultimately dismissed on summary judgment. It must be noted that the lawsuit was not dismissed on substantive grounds, but instead because Plaintiff's key witness, Lyle Preest, had died during the pendency of the litigation before his deposition was taken. Since Lyle Preest was the only witness who could testify as to the allegedly false statements made by the Defendants, the case was dismissed.

e. The Plaintiff's claims were never substantively considered in the prior case, and the lawsuit was against a different party (SANTANDER BANK) than the parties in this case (although PETER TRIANO was originally named as a party Defendant in the original suit, he was not a party at the time the case was disposed).

3

(Fig. 22 page 4)

All other bases for summary judgment were denied, No attorneys
fees were awarded.

e.   This lawsuit does not require the testimony of Lyle Preest. This
lawsuit is not based on fraud or misrepresentations made by
SOVEREIGN BANK or SANTANDER BANK, N.A. This
lawsuit is based on DIFFERENT misrepresentations made by
PETER TRIANO and LAWRENCE ROCHEFORT/AKERMAN
LLP, as described in more detail herein.

f.   The reason that the prior lawsuit is being mentioned in the
pleadings is to prepare the Court for the Defendants' claim in this
matter that this case is barred under the legal doctrine of *res
judicata*. This lawsuit is against DIFFERENT DEFENDANTS,
involves DIFFERENT CLAIMS, and invokes DIFFERENT
LEGAL THEORIES for liability. The doctrine of *res judicata* has
no applicability in this matter.

8.   The crux of this lawsuit is based on the claim that that PETER TRIANO and
LAWRENCE ROCHEFORT purposely misrepresented to Plaintiffs that
SANTANDER BANK, N.A. lacked the authority to consider any type of loan
modification or even allow reinstatement when in fact they knew the opposite to
be true.

a.   In fact, LAWRENCE ROCHFORT went so far as to allege
to Plaintiffs' counsel that Fannie Mae "would not allow"

4

139

(Fig. 22 page 5)

        SANTANDER BANK, N.A. to permit a reinstatement of

        the loans "under any circumstances." This was a flat-out

        misrepresentation, and is even inconsistent with the sworn

        testimony of PETER TRIANO in the prior litigation.

9.   Fannie Mae would not and could not take the position that a borrower is not

      permitted to reinstate "under any circumstances" as such a position is inconsistent

      with the **MANDATORY** FANNIE MAE 2010 SERVICING GUIDE UPDATE

      PART VII and PART VIII.

10.   The initial misrepresentation made by LAWRENCE ROCHEFORT /

      AKERMAN LLP was made in July, 2011.

        a.   Defendants will therefore argue that this claim is barred by the

              statute of limitations, given that claims "aiding or abetting fraud"

              or "civil conspiracy" must be filed within four (4) years, and this

              case was not filed until November, 2016.

        b.   However, Florida recognizes the "delayed discovery doctrine"

              when a victim of fraud has not yet learned that he has been

              victimized. There are times when a person is unable to discover

              that they have been injured. For example, fraud that is concealed

              and is not easily discoverable that can only be detected at a later

              time. It wouldn't be fair or reasonable to require the injured party

              to file a lawsuit when they could not have detected the injury. As a

              result, in some instances the Florida statute of limitations begins to

5

(Fig. 22 page 6)

          run from the time the injured party discovers or should have discovered that they have been injured.

c.   The Florida Legislature has stated that a cause of action accrues or begins to run when the last element of the cause of action occurs. An exception is made for claims of fraud in which the accrual of the causes of action is delayed until the plaintiff either knows or should know that the last element of the cause of action occurred.

d.   In fact, the absolute deadline for a fraud lawsuit is 12 years. See *F.S. 95.031(2)(a)*, which states, in pertinent part, that "...[a]n action for fraud under s. 95.11(3) must be begun within the period prescribed in this chapter, with the period running from the time the facts giving rise to the cause of action were discovered *or should have been discovered with the exercise of due diligence*, instead of running from any date prescribed elsewhere in s. 95.11(3), but in any event an action for fraud under s. 95.11(3) must be begun *within 12 years after the date of the commission of the alleged fraud, regardless of the date the fraud was or should have been discovered*." *(Emphasis added)*.

11.   Plaintiff has filed this lawsuit within four (4) years of the time that he discovered, or reasonably should have discovered the fraud. Plaintiff first obtained a copy of the *MANDATORY* FANNIE MAE 2010 SERVICING GUIDE UPDATE PART VII and PART VIII in 2016. It must be noted that this guide was requested in

6

(Fig. 22 page 7)

the prior litigation, but was never provided until Plaintiff was able to obtain same in his through his own research.

12. The initial misrepresentation made by LAWRENCE ROCHEFORT / AKERMAN LLP was made during the pendency of certain foreclosure actions that were filed in the Circuit Court of Lee County, Florida, Case Numbers 10-CA-060339 and 10-CA-060342 against the Plaintiffs.

    a.   Defendants will seek to avoid liability because the statement in question was made during the pendency of litigation and will seek the shield of the "litigation privilege."

    b.   Florida has long recognized a "litigation privilege" affording absolute immunity for communications made during the course of judicial proceedings, *unless the statements bear no relation to the proceeding or are fraudulently made for the sole purpose of inducing settlement.*

    c.   At the time the statement was made, LAWRENCE ROCHEFORT / AKERMAN LLP was trying to pressure the Plaintiff into reaching a settlement to the foreclosure cases. The sole purpose of the misrepresentation was to induce settlement.

13. Mediation was held on June 2, 2011 and the parties reached an agreement in principle. The specific agreement is not listed here in light of the mediation privilege. NO SPECIFIC STATEMENTS ABOUT WHAT HAPPENED AT MEDIATION ARE INCLUDED IN THIS AMENDED COMPLAINT. The written agreement was prepared by LAWRENCE ROCHEFORT and

7

(Fig. 22 page 8)

AKERMAN LLP after the mediation.

14. The "settlement documents" tendered by LAWRENCE ROCHEFORT and AKERMAN LLP were entirely inconsistent with the agreement in principle reached at the mediation.

15. Despite the mediation privilege, as set forth in *F.S. §44.405*, PETER TRIANO and LAWRENCE ROCHEFORT disclosed to 3rd parties that Plaintiff had agreed to settle at mediation.

16. PETER TRIANO and LAWRENCE ROCHEFORT falsely alleged to 3rd parties that Plaintiff ultimately rescinded his consent to settle that was allegedly provided at mediation.

17. In addition to being a false representation of the true facts (an agreement in principle was made, and then a settlement was drafted which was entirely inconsistent with such agreement), such disclosures were in violation of Florida law.

18. Ultimately, Fannie Mae was able to obtain final judgments in foreclosure against the apartment complexes, and then to assign the final judgments in foreclosure to SANTANDER BANK, N.A. prior to the foreclosure sales.

19. SANTANDER BANK, N.A. thereafter made assignments of its interests in the actions, with SANTANDER BANK, N.A.'s apparent assignees receiving title to the properties after successful credit bids at the sales, with the CROIX apartment complex at a high bid of $400,100.00, and the PEPPERTREE apartment complex at a high bid of $860,100.00.

8

143

(Fig. 22 page 9)

20. Upon information and belief, PETER TRIANO, LAWRENCE ROCHEFORT and AKERMAN LLP then profited from the sale of the loan or property to a third party, as it is believed that the Defendants have received the rights and interest to the judgments on the mortgage loans at less than fair market value, then sold them shortly thereafter at substantial profits.

    a. Plaintiff attempted to uncover the truth of these serious accusations by attempting to take the depositions of LAWRENCE ROCHEFORT and representative of Fannie Mae in the prior litigation. Such efforts were stymied by opposing counsel and the federal government.

    b. Plaintiff cannot conceive of any reason why Defendants would make the misrepresentations described herein unless there was some basis to personally profit from their deception.

    c. Discovery in this case will allow the Plaintiff to determine whether this allegation can be proven, but Plaintiff is operating in good faith in pursuing this matter. Uncovering corruption and fraud is not easy nor is it pleasant. Plaintiff will not be intimidated in his quest to uncover the truth.

21. The CROIX apartment complex was sold to a third party for $1,195,000.00.

22. The PEPPERTREE apartment complex was sold to a third party for $2,300,000.00.

23. Each sale price was well in excess of the principal balances of the respective mortgage loan.

24. Upon information and belief, in addition to the profits made on the sale of the

9

(Fig. 22 page 10)

CROIX apartment complex and the PEPPERTREE apartment complex, Fannie Mae also was able to recover the difference between the total amount owed against each complex and the sale prices at the foreclosure sales from the federal government under the TARP Relief program. In other words, Fannie Mae was made whole (including exorbitant attorney fees and default interest) at the expense of the taxpayers, and then, despite the alleged losses, the properties were resold weeks later for a 7 figure profit.

25.   Upon information and belief, LAWRENCE ROCHEFORT, AKERMAN LLP, and PETER TRIANO actually received much or all of the profit derived from the ultimate sale of the CROIX apartment complex and the PEPPERTREE apartment complex. That was the financial motivation for the fraudulent, misleading, and unlawful actions of the Defendants as described herein.

26.   Prior to the filing of this Amended Complaint, Plaintiff was served with 2 motions for sanctions, which alleged that Plaintiff's had made claims for relief based on agreements barred by F.S. 697.0304. Plaintiff has reviewed Florida Statute 687.0304, and has determined in good faith that said statute has no bearing on this case. Plaintiff is not suing out of a "credit agreement." Plaintiff's suit is for fraud and civil conspiracy arising out of material misstatements. Furthermore, to the extent there ever were any credit agreements related to this matter, such agreements were in writing.

27.   During his deposition in the prior litigation (which took place on August 15, 2015, far less than 4 years ago), PETER TRIANO swore that he had

10

(Fig. 22 page 11)

attempted to communicate with Plaintiff and had even visited the CROIX apartment complex and the PEPPERTREE apartment complex during the so-called loss mitigation process.

a.   However, PETER TRIANO also admitted that he had never made an appointment to view the apartment complexes (so PETER TRIANO alleged that he flew from New York to Florida for the sole purpose of viewing the apartments complexes, did so without appointments, and then returned to New York when FRANK LATELL was apparently unavailable to show him the apartment complexes).

b.   At all material times, FRANK LATELL was easy to reach, and there is no record of the alleged visits in either Plaintiff's records or the records of SOVEREIGN BANK or SANTANDER BANK, N.A.

c.   Upon information and belief, the assertions made by PETER TRIANO regarding his alleged loss mitigation efforts were outright manufactured lies.

28.   All conditions precedent to the filing of this action have been satisfied or waived.

COUNT I – AIDING AND ABETTING FRAUD
(Against all Defendants)

29.   This is an action for damages in excess of $15,000.00.

30.   Plaintiff re-alleges and re-avers paragraphs one (1) through twenty eight (28) as if fully set forth herein.

31.   This is an action seeking "in-concert" liability against a lawyer and a law firm in connection with their representation of a client or clients. In

11

(Fig. 22 page 12)

addition, this action seeks "in-concert" liability against PETER TRIANO, as an employee of SANTANDER BANK, N.A. for actions and statements he made in connection with his employment, but constituted intentional torts.

32. In the civil context, this type of claim leads to liability for those who help other actors or a main actor (usually for lawyers it is the client) to commit some tort against a third party. In practice, this often involves a claim that the lawyer helped the client either commit a fraud on a third party or breach some duty (usually a fiduciary duty) to a third party.

32. Aid and abet means simply to encourage, counsel, advise or assist in the commission of an act. The words comprehend all assistance rendered by the acts or words of encouragement or support or presence actual or constructive, to render assistance should it become necessary. It means to assent to an act; to end to it countenance and approval, either by an active participation in it or by in some manner advising encouraging it. The word 'abet' includes the element of knowledge of the wrongful purpose of the perpetrator and counsel and encouragement in the illegal act while the word 'aid' means to assist, to support the efforts of another.

33. When LAWRENCE ROCHEFORT (acting in his capacity as an employee or part owner of AKERMAN LLP) alleged that Fannie Mae would "not allow him to reinstate under any circumstances," LAWRENCE ROCHEFORT knowingly made a false statement of material fact. Not

12

(Fig. 22 page 13)

only was such a position forbidden by FANNIE MAE 2010 SERVICING

GUIDE UPDATE PART VII and PART VIII, but, upon information and

belief, there were no communications between LAWRENCE

ROCHEFORT and Fannie Mae during which time any such directive was

made or even implied.

34.   When PETER TRIANO disclosed (falsely) of what had been said and

what had occurred in mediation to 3rd parties, PETER TRIANO violated

the mediation privilege and made false statements of material fact.

35.   When LAWRENCE ROCHEFORT (acting in his capacity as an employee

or part owner of AKERMAN LLP) refused to respond to a Qualified

Written Request by falsely alleging that his client was not required to

respond, LAWRENCE ROCHEFORT knowingly made a false statement

of material fact.

     a.   The "litigation privilege" does not allow attorneys to disregard the

        Rules Regulating the Florida Bar.

     b.   See Rule 4-1-2(d) of the Rules Regulating the Florida Bar entitled

        "Objectives and Scope of Representation" which forbids lawyers

        from assisting a client in conduct known to be fraudulent. See also

        Rule 4-3.4 of the Rules Regulating the Florida Bar entitled

        "Fairness To Opposing Parties and Counsel."

36.   When PETER TRIANO swore under oath that he had made "several

attempts" to communicate with Plaintiff and had visited the CROIX and

13

148

(Fig. 22 page 14)

PEPPERTREE apartment complexes, he knowingly made false statements of material fact (and did so under oath under penalty of perjury).

37. The false statements of material facts and the violation of the mediation Privilege described herein evidence the existence of an underlying tort. Such false statements were designed to induce the reliance of Plaintiff and his counsel, and in fact, did induce such reliance. IT IS NOT OBJECTIVELY UNREASONABLE TO RELY ON THE FACTUAL STATEMENTS OF AN OFFICER OF THE COURT, EVEN IF IT IS A LAWYER REPRESENTING AN OPPOSING PARTY. Lawyers are held to a higher standard.

38. As a result, Plaintiff suffered substantial damages (to wit: the loss of the CROIX and PEPPERTREE apartment complexes, which had over a million dollars in equity). The false statements about what had happened at mediation stymied Plaintiff's attempts to seek justice through other channels.

39. Defendants had knowledge of the underlying torts described herein.

40. Defendants provided substantial assistance in the commission of the underlying torts described herein by affirmatively assisting, helping, concealing and/or by virtue of failing to act when required to do so, enabling the fraud to proceed and such actions proximately caused the harm described herein.

41. A person who aids and abets a tortfeasor is himself liable for the resulting

14

149

(Fig. 22 page 15)

harm to a third person. Aiding and abetting liability does not require the existence of, nor does it create, a pre-existing duty of care. Rather, aiding and abetting liability is based on proof of a scienter. The Defendants must *know* that the conduct they are aiding and abetting is a tort. Plaintiff alleges that the Defendants had the requisite knowledge in this case.

42. The Defendants knew that the misstatements described herein were false, and were made for the sole purpose of tricking the Plaintiff accepting a settlement and ultimately resulting in the loss of Plaintiff's equity in the CROIX and PEPPERTREE apartment complexes.

43. Plaintiff intends to make a showing to the Court that Plaintiff's claim should include punitive damages within the meaning of F.S. §768.72.

WHEREFORE, Plaintiff, FRANK LATELL prays that this Honorable Court enter Judgment in his favor, against Defendants, AKERMAN LLP, a Florida Limited Liability Partnership, LAWRENCE ROCHEFORT, individually, and PETER TRIANO, individually, for compensatory damages in an amount consistent with the evidence, the cost of litigation, interest, reasonable attorneys' fees, and such other and further relief as the Court deems appropriate under the circumstances (including punitive damages if applicable).

COUNT II – CIVIL CONSPIRACY
(Against all Defendants)

44. This is an action for damages in excess of $15,000.00.

45. Plaintiff re-alleges and re-aver paragraphs one (1) through twenty eight (28) as if fully set forth herein.

15

(Fig. 22 page 16)

46. This is a claim for civil conspiracy.

47. As alleged herein, the Defendants in this case worked together in an effort to trick the Plaintiff into forfeiting the equity in the CROIX and PEPPERTREE apartment complexes by convincing the Plaintiff into:

   a. Falsely acting "as if" meaningful loss mitigation was available and/or even being attempted; and

   b. Falsely describing what happened at mediation to 3rd parties (which would be a violation of the mediation privilege, even if such statements had been truthful) in an effort to impugn Plaintiff's credibility.

48. The foregoing constitutes a corrupt agreement between two or more parties.

49. The false statements and other acts described in Count I of this Complaint.

50. The Defendants' participation in the furtherance the plan or purpose of depriving Plaintiff of the CROIX and PEPPERTREE apartment complexes was intentional.

51. Plaintiff suffered damage or injury as a result, to wit: the loss of the CROIX and PEPPERTREE apartment complexes.

52. The Courts of this state have clearly held that a cause of action for civil conspiracy exists if "...the basis for the conspiracy is an independent wrong or tort which would constitute a cause of action if the wrong were done by one person." *Rivers v. Dillards Dept. Store*, 698 So. 2d 1328,

16

(Fig. 22 page 17)

1333 (Fla. 1ˢᵗ DCA 1997). *See also Liappas v. Augoustis*, 47 So. 2d 582 (Fla.1950) ("the gist of a civil action is not the conspiracy itself but the civil wrong which is done pursuant to the conspiracy and which results in damage to the plaintiff.")

52. Plaintiff intends to make a showing to the Court that Plaintiff's claim should include punitive damages within the meaning of F.S. §768.72.

WHEREFORE, Plaintiff, FRANK LATELL, prays that this Honorable Court enter Judgment in his favor, against Defendants, AKERMAN LLP, a Florida Limited Liability Partnership, LAWRENCE ROCHEFORT, individually, and PETER TRIANO, individually, for compensatory damages in an amount consistent with the evidence, the cost of litigation, interest, reasonable attorneys' fees, and such other and further relief as the Court deems appropriate under the circumstances (including punitive damages if applicable).

CERTIFICATE OF SERVICE

I HEREBY CERTIFY that a true and correct copy of the foregoing was furnished via regular U.S. Mail to Frank Latell, 5422 Peppertree Drive, Fort Myers, Florida 33908 (and via e-mail to latellf@hotmail.com), Theodore Tripp, Esq., 2400 First Street, Suite 300, Fort Myers, FL 33901 (and via e-mail to ttripp@hahnlaw.com, roliver@hahnlaw.com, FL-eservice@hahnlaw.com, jhyatt@hahnlaw.com, and jnavarrete@hahnlaw.com) and Robert Soriano, Esq. (counsel for PETER TRIANO), 4830 West Kennedy Boulevard, Suite 600, Tampa, FL 33609 (and via e-mail to Rsoriano@robsorianolaw. com) on this _18ᵗʰ_ day of _November_ , 2016.

MATTHEW S. TOLL, ESQ.
Florida Bar No.: 0785741
TOLL LAW
Attorneys for FRANK LATELL
1217 Cape Coral Parkway E., #121

17

(Fig. 22 page 18)

Cape Coral, Florida 33904
(239) 257-1743 (telephone)
(239) 257-1794 (facsimile)
matt@matthewtoll.com

March 16, 2007 my complaint was dismissed due to the Florida 4-year Statute of Limitations.

Now I ask myself: Why did my attorney file in the Florida Circuit Court? The Fannie Mae 2010 Servicing Guide Update Part VII and Part VIII ('Smoking Gun') was found shortly after the summary Judgement in the U.S. Federal Court. This new evidence should allow me to refile my complaint, against the conspiracy of Fannie Mae, Santander Bank and Ackerman for stealing U.S. Government Taxes, in the U.S. Federal Court.

My story should not end with a dismissed complaint.

Chapter 29: Kill Fannie Mae; the True Extent of *Their Fraud*

Peter Triano's resume stated that as Vice-President, Debt Management and Recovery (CRE-NY Workout Division) Sovereign Bank/Santander U.S.A. from August, 2008 through July, 2011, he managed a $300 million portfolio of non-performing commercial real estate loans (35-50) consisting of multi-family, office, and retail properties. During his deposition, Triano stated that one-half of these serviced loans were Fannie Mae.

The Fannie Mae portfolio is estimated at $150 million (one-half of $300 million).

The combined Latell properties original loans of $2.5 million (paid down to $2,337,268.05) generated a foreclosure court judgment penalty of $1,454,637.44 (called a loss but anyone in their right mind knows it is a profit) inclusive of 25 percent default interest and $368,793.54 prepayment penalty. It is estimated that the loan servicer, Triano, due to the 20 +/- Fannie Mae serviced loans, created a false loss to Fannie Mae. Assuming that the scheme was applied to all serviced properties in Santander Banks Fannie Mae portfolio, the following applies:

$1,454,637.44 (profit on Latell loans) divided by $2,500,000

(Latell loans) multiplied by $150,000,000 (Triano portfolio of Fannie Mae loans) equals $87,278,246.40 (Fannie Mae profit).

The combined court judgment of the Latell loans was $3,791,905.49 and the combined foreclosure sale was $1,260,200. The taxpayer got stuck for the difference in the amount of $2,531,705.49. It is estimated that the loan servicer, Triano, due to the 20 +/- Fannie Mae serviced loans, cost the taxpayer:

$2,531,705.49 divided by $2,500,000 (Latell loans) multiplied by $150,000,000 (Triano portfolio of Fannie Mae loans) equals $151,902,329.40 (bailout from the taxpayer).

The combined Santander Bank profit of the Latell properties was $2,234,800. It is estimated that Santander Bank made a profit of servicing Fannie Mae loans in Southwest Florida of: $2,234,800 divided by $2,500,000 (Latell loans) multiplied by $150,000,000 (Triano portfolio of Fannie Mae loans) equals $134,088,000.

It is beyond my ability to find out how much of the $116,149,000,000 (Propublica) taxpayer bailout was profit. My hope is to ultimately pursue this information and assist the U.S. taxpayer through a False Claims Act claim.

Fannie Mae employees personally involved in my "Latell" loans knew the rules of engagement, namely the "Fannie Mae 2010 Servicing Guide Update Part VII and Part VIII." The two Fannie Mae personnel who attended the mediation (from afar) stayed silent.

Fannie Mae Resource Center (Ron) who hesitantly stated "yes" to my question: "Would FNMA (Fannie Mae) rather foreclose on us and come after me personally for about a $2,000,000 deficiency than simply reinstate the loan and not suffer loss of principle?"

Carlus Flowers, Government and Industry Relations, Fannie Mae who responded five times to two U.S. Senators and one U.S. Congressman what Sovereign/Santander Bank (the loans servicer) told him without verifying (never contacted me).

This situation needed further investigation. Taxpayer government money was stolen. The best investigative service in the world and part of our government should and are required to investigate my complaint.

Three letters of complaint regarding Fannie Mae and its loan servicer, Sovereign Bank, were sent to the Federal Bureau of Investigation (FBI) dated August 15 and 24, 2011 and July 13, 2012. On August 6, 2012, I called the FBI; they responded that my complaint was being reviewed. On August 14, 2012, I received a call from the FBI that they would not pursue this case.

The FBI can get the evidence in stealing of taxpayer money (Fannie Mae employees included) and prosecute.

Wake up!

Chapter 30: Violation of the "Mediation Confidentiality and Privilege Act"

What happens in Vegas stays in Vegas - well not if you're an 'uomo ordinario,' ordinary man, like myself.

At the foreclosure mediation, the court-ordered mediation officer (attorney) spent the first 15 minutes explaining the workings of mediation and "whatever happens in the mediation stays in the mediation." The proposed 35-page settlement agreement (presented 2 weeks after the mediation, nothing provided, nothing signed at the mediation) was not accepted (not signed) so why and how did FHFA and others ever hear about it?

For example, I have received eight (8) separate written cor-respondences regarding the mediation and the proposed settlement agreement:

1 letter from FHFA, 5 responses from Fannie Mae via my state Congressman and Senators and 2 letters from Sovereign/ Santander Bank.

All are in violation of Florida Statute 44.401-44.406 known as the "Mediation Confidentiality and Privilege Act," which is defined as a protected and trusted relationship between parties.

During this entire process, trust me, I have not felt protected!

Chapter 31: "Too Big to Fail, So Big to Get Away with Fraud"

After 3 months of no response from 700 pre-publication editions sent to those of authority and the news media regarding this exposed Fannie Mae fraud, I have filed a complaint with the Consumer Financial Protection Bureau (CFPB).

Who is the CFPB?

Wikipedia states:

The Consumer Financial Protection Bureau is an agency of the United States Government responsible for consumer protection in the financial sector. CFPB jurisdiction includes banks, credit unions, securities firms, payday lenders, mortgage-servicing operations, foreclosure relief services, debt collectors and other financial companies operating in the United States.

The CFPB's creation was authorized by the Dodd-Frank Wall Street Reform and Consumer Protection Act, whose passage in 2010 was a legislative response to the financial crisis of 2007-08 and the subsequent Great Recession.

According to Director Richard Cordray, the Bureau's priorities are mortgages, credit cards and student loans. It was designed to consolidate employees and responsibilities from a number of other federal regulatory bodies, including the Federal Reserve, the Federal Trade Commission, the Federal Deposit Insurance Corporation, the National Credit Union Administration and even the Department of Housing and Urban Development. The Bureau is an independent unit located inside and funded by the United States Federal Reserve, with interim affiliation with the U.S. Treasury Department. The CFPB writes and enforces rules for financial institutions, examines both bank and non-bank financial institutions, monitors and reports on markets, as well as collects and tracts consumer complaints. Furthermore, as required under Dodd-Frank and outlined in the 2013 CFPB-State Supervisory Coordination Framework, the CFPB works closely with state regulators in coordinating supervision and enforcement activities.

I have given you facts: Fannie Mae and their loan servicer have committed fraud to steal the Latell properties and taxpayer money.

In 2017, 4 letters were sent to the Consumer Financial Protection Bureau dated April 10, May 22, June 2 and July 24.

It was made known to the CFPB that the finding of the Fannie Mae 2010 Servicing Guide Update Part VII and Part VIII became the 'smoking gun' to the conspiracy of the lies told by the Fannie Mae loan servicer (Santander National Bank), the smoke screen of the Fannie Mae foreclosure attorney (Akerman) and the silence of the Fannie Mae representatives at the 2011 foreclosure mediation.

My letter to the CFPB of June 2, 2017 was to add Santander National Bank (f/k/a Sovereign National Bank) and Akerman (f/k/a Akerman Senterfitt) as co-conspirators with Fannie Mae in the recently filed complaint.

I informed the CFPB of the federal statute of limitations (United States Department of Justice, Office of the United States

Attorneys, 650. Length of Limitations Period, Section 3293 of Title 18, United States Code). This document provides for a 10-year statute of limitations for financial institutions offenses, which involve violations of conspiracy to violate Title 18 of the United States Code.

Additionally, I informed the CFPB and made clear that since I now know that Fannie Mae was the perpetrator of this conspiracy affecting every American taxpayer, it is CFPB's responsibility to pursue this crime.

It was made known to the CFPB that because of my lawsuit (Complaint in the Federal Court), I have disclosures, interrogatories, affidavits and depositions regarding this conspiracy. My letters to the CFPB stated that further depositions must be taken of:

Peter Triano (Santander National Bank)
Lawrence Rochefort (Akerman)
Elizabeth McCloud (Fannie Mae)
Josh Rose (Fannie Mae)
Ron _____ (Fannie Mae Resource Center)
Frank Latell

Getting no information except that the status of my complaint was open, on July 20, 2017, I called and had a telephone talk with the CFPB. What I understood from this conversation was that the CFPB was trying to decide what to do with my complaint. In a follow-up letter of July 24, 2017, I asked that I would appreciate a response regarding if the CFPB was to take any action.

I got my answer:

(Fig. 23 CFPB Response; August 9, 2017)

From: CFPB
Sent: Wednesday, August 9, 2017 5:26 PM
To: latellf@hotmail.com
Subject: Please contact Other Government Agency or Office about your complaint.

Please contact Other Government Agency or Office about your complaint.

08/09/2017

Hello,

Thank you for your complaint 170601-2132790 about Fannie Mae.

After our review, we found that the best agency to help you with your issue is the Other Government Agency or Office. Please contact them about your issue. You can find the correct contact information for this agency by going to www.consumerfinance.gov/agencies.

Summary of your complaint

Complaint number: 170601-2132790
Date submitted to CFPB: 06/01/2017
Product: Mortgage
Issue: Struggling to pay mortgage

If you have questions for us, visit consumerfinance.gov or call (855) 411-2372 to speak with someone.

———

I want you to get the picture of our government in action. Upon contacting the U.S. Department of Justice, Office of the Inspector General on May 21, 2018, I received this response: "Our office does not have jurisdiction regarding the matter you describe. Therefore, as a courtesy, your complaint has been forwarded to the Consumer Financial Protection Bureau (CFPB)."

June 11, 2018, I sent a letter to the CFPB stating, "Doing what you said, I contacted the U.S. Department of Justice, office of the Inspector General. This Agency has forwarded my complaint to you. You have a responsibility to investigate my complaint."

The CFPB response by email of July 2, 2018 was: "After reviewing your complaint, it appears the Consumer Finance Protection Bureau cannot pursue the issue you describe. CFPB does not have any jurisdiction over any Local, State or Federal Government Agency."

Note: Fannie Mae, Santander National Bank and Akerman are not government agencies.

(Fig. 24 CFPB Response July 2, 2018)

From: CFPB Consumer Response
Sent: Monday, July 2, 2018 3:04 PM
To: latellf@hotmail.com
Subject: Case 180612-3232213 { ref:_00Do0HJvn._500t0AwOEH:ref }

Thank you for contacting the Consumer Financial Protection Bureau (CFPB).

After reviewing your complaint, it appears the Consumer Financial Protection Bureau cannot pursue the issue you described. CFPB does not have any jurisdiction over any Local, State or Federal Government Agency.

Thank You,

Consumer Response Team | Office of Consumer Response
Office: (855) 411-CFPB (2372)
Bureau of Consumer Financial Protection
consumerfinance.gov

Confidentiality Notice: If you received this email by mistake, you should notify the sender of the mistake and delete the e-mail and any attachments. An inadvertent disclosure is not intended to waive any privileges.
ref:_00Do0HJvn._500t0AwOEH:ref

Think about it:

CFPB

Consumer - you and I

Financial - yep, fits the bill

Protection - preventing harm or injury

Bureau - for US citizens

Why was the Consumer Finance Protection Bureau hiding from the obvious reason of their creation? Is this the DEEP STATE? Who is able to pull the strings of the CFPB?

The CFPB is a failed Agency.

Chapter 32: Another Failed Agency, the Conservator

I want to inform you about my experience with another government agency.

Fannie Mae and Freddie Mac faced a series of accounting and financial problems, which led many in Congress to conclude that there was a need for a stronger regulator. The Housing and Economic Recovery Act (HERA) of 2008, created the Federal Housing Finance Agency (FHFA) to be the regulator for the housing Government Sponsored Enterprises (GSEs).

From Wikipedia, the free encyclopedia:

The Federal Housing Finance Agency (FHFA) is an independent federal agency created as the successor regulatory agency of the Federal Housing Finance Board (FHFB), the Office of Federal Housing Enterprise Oversight (OFHEO), and the U.S. Department of Housing and Urban Development government-sponsored enterprise mission team, absorbing the powers and regulatory authority of both entities, with expanded legal and regulatory authority, including the ability to place Government Sponsored Enterprises (GSEs) into receivership or conservatorship.

In its role as regulator, it regulates Fannie Mae, Freddie Mac, and the 11 Federal Home Loan Banks (FHL Banks, or FHL Bank Systems). It is wholly separate from the Federal Housing Administration, which largely provides mortgage insurance.

The FHFA was created for the conservatorship of Fannie Mae and the other GSEs. Its role as conservator was to regulate and oversee the operations of the GSEs. Along with other government agencies, I sent letters to the FHFA and the FHFA, OIG (Office of the Inspector General). I considered these agencies to have the authority and responsibility to protect borrowers from misrepresentations, bullying, fraud and non-compliance with federal law.

The FHFA, OIG responded that they would pass it on to the FHFA. The FHFA responded that I had reneged on a verbal agreement.

There was a 35-page document presented 15 days after our mediation, which was not part of the mediation (verbal agreement). My attorney's (John Agnew) response to the document states that he would have to red line through more than one-half of it (Chapter 10). As to a verbal agreement, Chapter 30 tells of violations of the "Mediation Confidentiality and Privilege Act."

I am in receipt of 2 letters from the FHFA dated October 31, 2011 and February 7, 2012, both stating that "FHFA has no regulatory authority over Sovereign Bank," the servicer of Fannie Mae loans. As stated above, the FHFA was created to have regulatory authority over Fannie Mae and obviously Fannie Mae's loan servicer, Sovereign Bank. The FHFA letters are a perfect example of pushing paper and not knowing, understanding or caring why said agency exists.

Did they not want to confront the thief or was it just plain old ignorance?

(Fig. 25 FHFA Letter; December 30, 2011)

Federal Housing Finance Agency
1700 G Street, N.W., Washington, D.C. 20552-0003
Telephone: (202) 414-3800
Facsimile: (202) 414-3823
www.fhfa.gov

December 30, 2011

Mr. Frank Latell
5422 Peppertree Drive
Fort Myers, FL 33908

RE: FHFA CCN#: 2011 10 21 007

Dear Mr. Latell:

As disclosed on our website, FHFA generally does not intervene in matters involving individual mortgages, property sales or transfers, foreclosure or other actions. The Enterprises each have a review process to look into situations that arise involving their mortgages or property transactions.

Upon our receipt of your September 14, 2011 letter (Edward DeMarco, Acting Director of FHFA was copied), FHFA forwarded it to Fannie Mae for further review and to work with you directly, if appropriate. Subsequently, Fannie Mae advised FHFA of the following:

- Your loans have been reviewed by the Fannie Mae Resource Center, Congressional Inquiries Office and the Multifamily Business. This is in addition to reviews conducted by your servicer, Sovereign Bank.
- You defaulted on your loans in April 2010. Foreclosure proceedings were initiated in October 2010.
- In June 2011, Fannie Mae, Sovereign Bank and you participated in a court-ordered mediation. A verbal agreement was reached whereby you agreed to not contest the foreclosure in exchange for releases of certain liabilities. However, after the necessary written Settlement Agreement was prepared and distributed for signatures, you chose not to execute the document.
- Your request for a loan modification was denied. The denial was provided to you in writing by both the servicer and Fannie Mae's Congressional Inquiries office.
- Fannie Mae issued Congressional letters that responded your concerns to Florida Senator Marco Rubio (August 12, 2011) and Congresswoman Connie Mack (August 12 and 31, 2011.)
- The loans remain in default. You have failed to perform under the mediated agreement. Through the servicer, Fannie Mae will continue to pursue its rights and remedies in accordance with the applicable loan documents and local law.

Sincerely,

Christine Eldarrat

Christine Eldarrat, Executive Advisor
Office of Congressional Affairs and Communications
Federal Housing Finance Agency (FHFA)

Frank Latell

(Fig. 26 FHFA Letter; October 31, 2011)

Federal Housing Finance Agency

1200 G Street, N.W., Washington, D.C. 20552-0003
Telephone: (202) 414-3800
Facsimile: (202) 414-3823
www.fhfa.gov

October 31, 2011

Mr. Frank Latell
5422 Peppertree Drive
Fort Myers, FL 33908

RE: FHFA CCN#: 2011 10 21 007

Dear Mr. Latell:

Thank you for contacting the Federal Housing Finance Agency, the regulator and conservator for Fannie Mae and Freddie Mac, and regulator for the Federal Home Loan Banks. Please be advised that FHFA has no regulatory authority over Sovereign Bank.

We are forwarding your information to Fannie Mae personnel for a more detailed review. As a result, they will contact you to discuss your concerns and to obtain additional information as needed. They will advise us of their communication with you and the resolution of your concern.

Sincerely,

Christine Eldarrat, Executive Advisor
Office of Congressional Affairs and Communications
Federal Housing Finance Agency (FHFA)

172

Chapter 33: SACRED COW - why?

All of 100 Senators and 435 House Members (elected to be responsible for US Government funds) were sent undeniable proof of the Fannie Mae crime of stealing taxpayer money. Notices were also sent to 300 individuals, watchdog agencies, news media, talk radio and law schools totaling over 835 with no takers or responses.

I ask myself, why did they refuse to look at undeniable proof of a US Government crime? No one has doubted my claim. And trust me, I've watched Godfather but still, why haven't the criminals tried to stop me?

Fannie Mae and the other GSEs (Government Sponsored Enterprises) own trillions of dollars of housing mortgages. Fannie Mae is by far the biggest of these GSEs.

The US Congress enacted the Housing Economic Recovery Act, HERA, authorizing the US Treasury to lend or invest unlimited amounts of money to the GSEs. This act established the Federal Housing Finance Agency, FHFA, to be the conservator of Fannie Mae. The FHFA has not only failed in its responsibility as conservator but Fannie Mae is able to operate under the guise of this conservatorship.

I've recently made known of this Fannie Mae crime to the

Inspector Generals of 12 Government Agencies. 6 have informed me as follows:

"...has no jurisdiction over the matter."

"The matters are outside our investigative jurisdiction."

"Complaint does not fall within our jurisdiction."

"Our office is not authorized..."

"...has no jurisdiction..."

"...has no jurisdiction or oversight..."

After 3 letters, (December 30, 2017 and February 12, 2018 certified) and (March 15, 2018 with enclosures), informing of undeniable proof, the following 6 Inspector Generals have not responded:

Department of Housing and Urban Development
Department of the Treasury
Federal Housing Finance Agency
Integrity Committee, Council of the Inspector Generals on Integrity and Efficiency
Small Business Administration
Treasury Inspector General for Tax Administration

The U.S. Department of Justice, Office of the Inspector General, by letter of May 21, 2018, has forwarded my complaint to the (obvious responsible agency) Consumer Financial Protection Bureau who has previously told me to, "Please contact other..."

Of the two letters (December 14, 2017 and March 14, 2018) I sent to (my representatives) Senators' Bill Nelson and Marco

Rubio and Congressman Francis Rooney and copies of the 3 letters sent to the Inspector Generals, only Senator Nelson responded. This response by letter of March 22, 2018 stated, "We have forwarded this and all pertinent information to the appropriate agency." By letter of March 27, 2018 Senator Nelson's staff informed me of the response from Fannie Mae (the accused perpetrator). Fannie Mae's response was only regarding the foreclosure, "Fannie Mae was not able to approve Mr. Latell for any work out retention options..." (fox guarding chickens).

Quite possibly I did not make myself clear regarding Lyle Preest (my finance officer) being told that the loans had to be forty-five days past due to discuss modification. My stopping payment and placing the exact payment amounts in a safe recovery place resulted in entrapment to put our properties in default. The loan servicer would not respond and foreclosed.

After eight years of being led into default of our properties through entrapment, lies, hidden and denied documentation, two lawsuits, no response or excuses from many to not get involved regarding my accusations of this Fannie Mae crime, I now believe Fannie Mae to be a 'SACRED COW.'

Merriam-Webster defines 'sacred cow' as 'one that is often unreasonably immune from criticism or opposition;' Dictionary. com's definition is, 'an individual, organization, institution, etc., considered to be exempt from criticism or questioning;' Wikipedia's definition is 'something considered (perhaps unreasonably) immune from question or criticism,' Webster's II New College Dictionary definition is, 'one immune from criticism or attack.'

A major crime has been committed, continues with Fannie Mae and requires US Government investigation. My hope is that through my writings, I can awaken the people of this country to call for action.

Chapter 34: Pulled Strings

Fannie Mae makes money by stringing out proceedings to a final Foreclosure Summary Judgment granting the principal due, a 25 percent default interest rate and a prepayment penalty.

From Peter Triano's portfolio, established through his resume and deposition, the taxpayer most likely got stuck for well over $100 million dollars through the Sovereign/Santander Bank servicing of Fannie Mae loans in Southwest Florida. Now multiply this by other areas of America serviced by Sovereign/Santander Bank and the number of agencies servicing Fannie Mae loans.

HERA was created to strengthen and unify oversight of the GSEs. The GSEs are comprised of Fannie Mae, Freddie Mac and 12 Federal Home Loan Banks. Fannie Mae's and Freddie Mac's total assets are 5-plus Trillion Dollars. We have 12 Federal Home Loan Banks with unknown, to this author, assets. TRILLIONS OF DOLLARS MAKES FANNIE MAE A 'SACRED COW.'

Do you remember Deep Throat - the Watergate scandal's key informant? Now we have Deep State - influential individuals who secretly control government policy.

Jerome Corsi's book, *Killing the Deep State: The Fight to Save President Trump* refers to the Deep State as the real Government of the United States, the players who pull the strings no matter who you vote for or who is in office.

Rush Limbaugh stated that the Deep State controls most who are pawns in both parties of Congress.

In my case, the no responses, no jurisdiction and the getting nowhere excuses of the many I have informed are in the classification, as Rush Limbaugh said, of pawns of the Deep State. It becomes obvious that Fannie Mae is operated within and protected by this Deep State.

Chapter 35: Undeniable Facts

The following are undeniable facts regarding the fraud and conspiracy by Fannie Mae, Fannie Mae loan servicer, Santander National Bank, and the Fannie Mae foreclosure law firm, Akerman:

Discovering the Fannie Mae 2010 Servicing Guide Update Part VII and Part VIII emphasized that Fannie Mae, the foreclosure lawyer and the loan servicer intentionally ignored, hid, lied and denied the said document.

Peter Triano, Sovereign/Santander Bank Vice President, Debt Management & Recovery Workout Officer of Fannie Mae loans, made a big mistake of assuming our loans to be in his category of other loans. From his sworn deposition of August 13, 2015, United States District Court, Fort Myers, Florida, page 73, lines 3-6, "I believe the value of those assets had declined significantly along with many assets in that southwest region."

Our Government was complacent by its involvement in the bailout of Fannie Mae through its creation of the Housing Economic Recovery Act. The Federal Housing Finance Agency was created to regulate Fannie Mae and other Government Sponsored Enterprises (GSEs). Rather than regulate, through its incompetency, the FHFA allowed Fannie Mae and their loan servicer to commit this crime of fraud.

In 2018, I wrote to several government agencies in care of their Inspector General's. On May 21, the US Department of Justice, Office of the Inspector General responded, "...as a courtesy, your complaint has been forwarded to the Consumer Financial Protection Bureau."

The Consumer Financial Protection Bureau was legislated into existence by the Dodd-Frank Bill of July 2010 to overhaul financial regulations and provide consumer protection in foreclosures of mortgage-servicing operations. I followed up to CFPB with my own correspondence detailing multiple, substantiated complaints. Their response was, "CFPB does not have jurisdiction over any Local, State or Federal Government Agency." Our complaint was not against a government agency. Our complaint was against a conspiracy of Fannie Mae, Santander National Bank and Akerman.

Furthermore, the Proposed Settlement Agreement offered by Fannie Mae's foreclosure attorney, Lawrence Rochefort of Akerman, was written in such a manner that I am exposed to additional liability. It required my wife and I to remain the owner and manager and for the foreclosure to continue without interference to achieve a monetary Court Judgment to, I believe, establish the bailout for Fannie Mae from the U.S. Government.

Fannie Mae's scheme was not to steal from us or any other property owner but to steal from the taxpayer. We and others are just a casualty. The incentive for the loan servicer, in our case Santander Bank, was to acquire those properties that are profitable, through the foreclosure sale. The incentive for the foreclosure attorney, in our case Akerman, was to get a piece of that profitability.

I believe that a sales price for the Croix Apartments in the amount of $1,195,000 was negotiated prior to the foreclosure sale to Sovereign Bank for $400,100.00. Peppertree Apartments was ultimately sold for $2,300,000.00 (three months after the foreclosure sale to Sovereign Bank for $860,000.00). The total profit to Sovereign/Santander Bank therefore appears to be no less than $2,234,800.00. The final judgment of both Latell properties includes the statement:

"The court retains jurisdiction of the action to grant such other and further relief as it deems just and proper, including without limitation issuing writs of possession, and a deficiency judgment, and an award of attorney's fees and costs to plaintiff."

It is important to note that neither Fannie Mae nor its loans servicer, Sovereign Bank, even bothered to pursue a deficiency or attorney fees. I believe that this was done because there were no true "deficiencies," it is alleged that Fannie Mae received a bailout for the combined judgments of $3,791,905.49 less the combined "sale prices" from foreclosure sales in the amount $1,260,200.00. This equals $2,531,705.49, courtesy of the U.S. taxpayer.

The combined judgment $3,791,905.49, less the loans combined principal $2,337,268.05, equals a profit to Fannie Mae of $1,454,637.44. That's right. I owed $2,337,268.05, but after all the default interest, the imposition of prepayment penalties and attorney's fees associated with the foreclosure actions, the total was increased to $3,791,905.49.

Let's summarize for a moment here, so that the true extent of what happened can really sink in. We owed approximately $2.3 million associated with the Latell Croix and Peppertree buildings. We were not in default. We sought loan modifications, but were told that in order to obtain same, we had to default. Based on this information, we defaulted. We kept the exact amount of what the loan payments were each month in a separate account, so all missed loan payments could be paid in full once the modifications were granted. After the defaults, we were never given any modification offers and were even denied the right to reinstate the loans. The $2.3 million in obligations were transmogrified into nearly $3.9 million in judgments through the foreclosure process. We believe that the difference, the so-called losses, were reimbursed by the federal government. The properties then appear to have been sold for a profit of an additional $2.3 million.

Now you understand. If the loans were reinstated, we would have paid the $2.3 million that was owed. By not allowing a reinstatement, much greater profits could be generated. Is this what Congress intended?

Chapter 36: They Stole *Your Money!*

All the evidence, all the false posturing, all distill down to 1 question:

Would Fannie Mae rather foreclose and come after me personally for a $2,000,000.00 deficiency rather than simply reinstate the loans and not suffer loss of principal?

Yes.

At first, I could not understand such an answer, but now I believe Fannie Mae preferred this route because only this route allowed for a bailout from the U.S. Government through the Housing Economic Recovery Act of 2008.

The extent of this scheme, I believe, is in the billions of taxpayer dollars; Fannie Mae was bailed out $116,149,000,000.

Our Government is intentionally ignoring this crime and giving Fannie Mae a pass. Additionally, Government agencies are asleep at the wheel and because of the 2020 Coronavirus outbreak, the theft of Government bailout tax money will happen again.

Personally, the foreclosure and our lawsuits in the Federal and the Circuit Court's cost us in excess of $100,000. Our complaint may be still prosecutable within the Federal Statute of Limitations.

Chapter 37: The False Claims Act and Qui Tam "Whistleblowing"

The False Claims Act is an American federal law that imposes liability on persons and companies who defraud government programs. The law includes a qui tam provision that allows people who are not affiliated with the government to file actions on behalf of the government called "whistleblowing."

The term "qui tam" refers to the Latin expression "qui tam pro domino rege quam pro se ipso in hae parte sequitur," which means, "who sues on behalf of the King as well as himself." The justification for allowing qui tam litigation was to encourage citizens to report wrongdoing against the government, wrongdoing that without the qui tam provision, would likely go unnoticed. In short, the government hoped that economic incentives (rewards) would promote private enforcement of federal legislation.

Providing ordinary Americans the ability to combat fraud, the False Claims Act helps recover damages, and to bring accountability to those who would take advantage of the American taxpayers.

The Fraud Enforcement and Recovery Act of 2009, or FERA, amends the federal criminal code to include, within the definition of "financial institution," a mortgage lending business or any person or entity that makes, in whole or part, a federally related mortgage loan and defines "mortgage lending business" as an organization that finances or refinances any debt secured by an interest in real estate, including private mortgage companies and their subsidiaries and whose activities affect interstate or foreign commerce.

FERA applies the prohibition against defrauding the federal government to fraudulent activities involving a federal economic stimulus, recovery, or rescue plan.

Now, ten-plus years into this crime, an excess of $100,000 in legal and other expenses, those in government (responsible for protecting taxpayer money) ignoring and hiding from this crime, and that it will happen again from the Coronavirus bailout, requires me to become a "whistleblower" under the qui tam provision of the False Claims Act.

Chapter 38: Who's Afraid of the Big Bad Wolf?

Over the following year, I contacted law firms who specialized in qui tam litigation and the False Claims Act; lawyers take these cases at no expense to the claimant unless the case is won.

Obviously, the law firm considering this case has to be very cautious considering charges of fraud are against a conspiracy of Fannie Mae, Santander Bank and the law firm of Akerman Senterfitt, LLP.

Wikipedia sheds some insight into these big-name companies.

Fannie Mae:

The Federal National Mortgage Association (FNMA), commonly known as Fannie Mae, is a United States Government Sponsored Enterprise (GSE) and, since 1968, a publicly traded company. The corporation's purpose is to "expand the secondary mortgage market by securitizing mortgage loans in the form of mortgage-backed securities, allowing lenders to reinvest their assets into more lending and in effect increasing the number of lenders in the mortgage market by reducing the reliance on locally based savings and loan associations.

"As of 2018, Fannie Mae is ranked number 21 on the Fortune 500 rankings of the largest United States corporations by total revenue."

Santander Bank:

Santander Bank, is a wholly owned subsidiary of the Spanish Santander Group, based in Boston and its principal market is the northeastern United States. Stats: Deposits $57.5 billion, 650 retail banking offices, 2,000 ATM's, employs @ 9,800. Offers: Corporate and retail banking, mortgages, insurance, financial management, credit card and capital markets.

Originally known as Sovereign Bank, on October 17, 2013 it was rebranded Santander Bank.

According to the Minority Corporate Counsel Association:

Akerman Senterfitt, LLP:

"Akerman Senterfitt is a premier, full-service law firm, specializing in corporate, labor and employment, litigation, and intellectual property work. In addition to newly opened offices in New York, Washington, DC, Northern Virginia, and Los Angeles, Akerman Senterfitt has a solid presence throughout Florida and is now the largest law firm in the state. In fact, the firm's client history dovetails with Florida state history: A firm partner was instrumental in the routing of Interstate 4 through the Orlando area, the procuring of land for Disney World, and the founding of Sun Banks, now SunTrust."

According to The National Law Review:

"With 650 attorneys and consultants in 24 offices, Akerman Senterfitt is distinguished by its comprehensive Corporate, Real Estate, Construction, Government Relations, Labor & Employment, Litigation, and IP practices. Providing services to local, regional, national and international clients, our team represents private and public companies, government entities, educational institutions and high net-worth individuals in over 40 different practice areas, and provide clients with not only sound legal advice but innovative and effective business solutions." natlawreview.com; March 8, 2022; Vol XII, Num 67

***

Of the law firms that I contacted, some did not respond, but of those who did, they specialized in medical fraud only and recommended other named firms. Some accepted my information but upon being presented to the firm's board were not accepted. Upon my questioning one firm of the fear of bringing charges against Fannie Mae, I got a reluctant positive response.

Chapter 39: The Department of UN-Justice

The Department of Justice issues guidance on False Claims Act matters:

Department of Justice

JUSTICE NEWS

Tuesday, May 7, 2019

The Civil Division today announced the release of formal guidance to the Department of Justice's False Claims Act litigators. The False Claims Act provides important remedies for fraud committed against the United States.

"The Department of Justice has taken important steps to incentivize companies to voluntarily disclose misconduct and cooperate with investigations; enforcement of False Claims Act is no exception," Assistant Attorney General Jody Hunt said. "False Claims Act defendants may merit a more favorable resolution by providing meaningful assistance to the Department of Justice – from voluntary disclosure, which is the most valuable form of cooperation, to various other efforts, including the sharing of information gleaned from an internal investigation and taking remedial steps through new or improved compliance programs."

On July 20, 2021, I sent the following letter to the U.S. Department of Justice, Office of Public Affairs:

(See Fig. 27)

July 20, 2021

Frank Latell
5422 Peppertree Drive
Fort Myers, Florida 33908

U. S. Department of Justice
Office of Public Affairs
950 Pennsylvania Avenue NW
Washington, DC 20530-0001

Dear Office of Public Affairs:

My qui tam, false claim whistleblowing is about the Fannie Mae loans servicer and attorney scheming to steal $150,000,000 federal tax money from the bailout to Fannie Mae provided by the Housing Economic Recovery Act of 2008. I've written the story of my true experience.

I filed in the Federal Court (representing myself) a lawsuit against Santander National Bank. After one year of my supposed lack of standing, 2 Court stays, trouble getting discovery etc., I contacted an attorney as my representative. Difficult discovery continued, some depositions were taken, some refused. After 2 ½ years, the defendant upon wanting to take the deposition of my finance officer (key witness), found him to be dead, resulting in a summary judgment closing my case.

Find enclosed a copy of my story and a short synopsis.

This information is provided in hopes that you will pursue this false claim against the government.

Sincerely,

Frank Latell
latellf@hotmail.com

193

Receiving no response from my July 20 letter, on September 6, 2021, I sent the following email to the Department of Justice, Office of Public Affairs, Civil Division. From September 6 until November 2, 2021 at 9:05 a.m., I sent 9 requests for a reply. I got my reply on November 2, 2021 at 1:25 p.m.

(Fig. 28 Begin on bottom of page 1 of 6-page attachment to read email thread. Then read pages 2 and 3 before returning to September 6, 2021 on page 1.)

(Fig. 28 page 1)

5th sending, please reply

Sent from Mail for Windows

From: Microsotf account team
Sent: Tuesday, September 28, 2021 1:59 PM
To: Civil.Feedback@usdoj.gov
Subject: RE: Qui Tam Whistleblower

4th sending, please reply.

Sent from Mail for Windows

From: Microsotf account team
Sent: Monday, September 20, 2021 11:36 AM
To: Civil.Feedback@usdoj.gov
Subject: RE: Qui Tam Whistleblower

Third sending, please reply.

Sent from Mail for Windows

From: Microsotf account team
Sent: Tuesday, September 14, 2021 10:41 AM
To: Civil.Feedback@usdoj.gov
Subject: FW: Qui Tam Whistleblower

Second sending:

Sent from Mail for Windows

From: Microsotf account team
Sent: Monday, September 6, 2021 2:44 PM
To: Civil.Feedback@usdoj.gov
Subject: Qui Tam Whistleblower

DOJ Civil Division:

July 20, I sent a packet containing a forwarding letter, my story and a short synopsis to your 950 Pennsylvania Ave NW, Washington DC address. A follow-up message to phone number 202 514 2007 on August 19 resulted in no response. This should be of upmost interest to you being the investigator and action taker of protecting the U. S. Government (tax payer) money.

(Fig. 28 page 2)

PART OF EMAIL OF SEPTEMBER 6, 2021

My qui tam whistleblowing is about the Fannie Mae loans servicer and the Fannie Mae attorney scheming to steal federal tax money from the bailout to Fannie Mae provided by the Housing Economic Recovery Act of 2008.

Nine years ago our rental properties were foreclosed. We lost our retirement income. This same scheme was used to steal $150,000,000 (most likely more) from the federal government (tax money) in South West Florida.

After the foreclosure I filed in the federal court, representing myself, a lawsuit against Santander National Bank. After one year of my supposed lack of standing, 2 court stays, trouble getting discovery, etc., I contacted an attorney as my representative. Difficult discovery continued, some depositions were taken, some refused. After 2 ½ years, the Defendant upon wanting to take the deposition of my finance officer (key witness) strangely found him to be dead resulting in a Summary Judgment closing the case.

Following is a short synopsis of my story:

Scheme occurred in SW Florida taking advantage of the 2008 housing crisis. Loans were in jeopardy resulting in a Fannie Mae U.S. Government bailout. Prior to the crisis many multi-family rental properties were bought at a high price, refinanced and being converted to condominiums for sale. This market failed leaving owners with over-financed rental properties in a weak renter market.

Santander National Bank was the servicer of 20 +/- SW Florida Fannie Mae mortgaged multi-family rental properties valued at approximately $150,000,000.

Rent loss was also my problem although I did not offer my properties for condo conversion and they were not over-financed.

Interest rates having dropped considerable, I was seeking a loan modification for a lower interest rate.

The scheme was between Peter Triano, the Santander Bank Fannie Mae loans servicer, and Lawrence Rochefort, the Akerman Senterfitt Fannie Mae attorney.

Seeking the loans modification (interest rate), my finance officer was informed in June of 2010 that the loans had to be 45 days in default to discuss loan modification. I did (entrapment).

Peter Triano then refused to talk to us. Lawrence Rochefort began the foreclosure.

Documentation regarding the loan servicing was requested. The foreclosure attorney and loans servicer would not provide, denied and lied that said documentation was privileged or non-existent.

After 14 months we went to mediation. My finance officer and I were there to negotiate a new interest rate on my $2,337,268.05 mortgaged properties. Peter Triano's only offer was to forgive the $1,100,000 penalty (25% interest, prepayment and attorney fees) and the foreclosure continues. I refused.

Triano's and Rochefort's scheme was to get a court judgment in as large an amount as possible to 'prove' a 'loss' to Fannie Mae and to allow Fannie Mae to be reimbursed by the bailout provided by the Housing Economic and Recovery Act of 2008 (HERA).

(Fig. 28 page 3)

PART OF EMAIL OF SEPTEMBER 6, 2021

Santander Bank, having 6 appraisals, bought the properties at the foreclosure sale and within 0 and 3 months had both properties sold for a profit of $2,224,800. Fannie Mae got a bailout of taxpayer money in the amount of $2,531,705.49 over and above the foreclosure sale amount of said properties. Of the other 20 +/- Fannie Mae mortgaged properties serviced by Santander Bank it is estimated that Fannie Mae received a bailout of taxpayer money from the Government of $150,000,000 +/-. Using my properties as a norm, Santander Bank made $150,000,000 +/- from foreclosure purchases and sales.

I filed a law suite contesting the foreclosure. This provided factual information through discovery. The deposition of Peter Triano provided great discovery and many lies. It was discovered that the loans servicer, Santander Bank, reported to Fannie Mae through a Service Workout Action Template (SWAT). Efforts to get copies resulted in only a SWAT time line. Stated, October 2010 "Servicer submitted SWAT stating that the borrower is nonresponsive. The servicer recommends commencing foreclosure".

I had lost touch with my finance officer. Upon efforts of the defendants to take his deposition, he was found to be dead. A summary judgment in favor of the defendant was issued because of the death of my finance officer (key witness).

Dying in a hospice care facility, my being suspicious, and knowing that he would have called me, upon inquiring, I could not get information.

Many efforts to get documentation of the working arrangements (service agreement) for Fannie Mae and the loans servicer resulted in failure. Shortly after the summery judgment was found the "Fannie Mae 2010 Servicing Guide Update Part VII and Part VIII" with a mandatory effective date of January 1, 2011. The Fannie Mae attorney foreclosed on our properties in gross violation of the delinquency and default prevention requirements of this document.

I believe that the Federal Statute of Limitations is 10 years.

Please respond,

Sincerely,

Frank Latell
latell@hotmail.com
239 985 2260

197

(Fig. 28 page 4)

From: Microsotf account team
Sent: Tuesday, November 2, 2021 9:05 AM
To: Civil.Feedback@usdoj.gov
Subject: RE: Qui Tam Whistleblower,

9th sending, please reply

Sent from Mail for Windows

From: Microsotf account team
Sent: Monday, October 25, 2021 1:20 PM
To: Civil.Feedback@usdoj.gov
Subject: RE: Qui Tam Whistleblower,

8th sending, please reply

Sent from Mail for Windows

From: Microsotf account team
Sent: Tuesday, October 19, 2021 3:33 PM
To: Civil.Feedback@usdoj.gov
Subject: RE: Qui Tam Whistleblower,

7th sending, please reply

Sent from Mail for Windows

From: Microsotf account team
Sent: Monday, October 11, 2021 11:28 AM
To: Civil.Feedback@usdoj.gov
Subject: RE: Qui Tam Whistleblower,

6th sending, please reply

Sent from Mail for Windows

From: Microsotf account team
Sent: Monday, October 4, 2021 2:43 PM
To: Civil.Feedback@usdoj.gov
Subject: RE: Qui Tam Whistleblower

(Fig. 28 Page 5)

From: Microsotf account team
Sent: Wednesday, November 3, 2021 10:32 AM
To: Feedback, Civil
Subject: RE: Qui Tam Whistleblower,

Dear DOJ Civil Division:

Thank you for finely responding.

It is not that I am seeking a qui tam reward , but that I am first hand reporting a scheme that has stolen a large sum of money from the American taxpayer along with our properties. You requiring me to get an attorney to continue pursuing this is B S. I've already spent over $100,000 in attorney fees over law suites pertaining to the stealing of our properties. I would think that you would want to discover the stealing of $150,000,000 (most likely more) of taxpayer money. I sent you my story via U. S. postal mail.

Sincerely,

Frank Latell
latellf@hotmail.com
239 985 2260

Sent from Mail for Windows

From: Feedback, Civil
Sent: Tuesday, November 2, 2021 1:25 PM
To: Microsotf account team
Subject: RE: Qui Tam Whistleblower,

Dear Mr. Latell:

Thank you for contacting the Department of Justice about the process of filing a *qui tam*, or whistleblower, lawsuit on behalf of the United States.

Your email indicates a desire to file a *qui tam*, or whistleblower, complaint on behalf of the Federal Government under the False Claims Act. The False Claims Act sets forth an established procedure for filing such claims that is intended, in part, to protect your whistleblower status. Among other things, the Act requires that all complaints be filed under seal in a United States District Court possessing proper venue. I invite you to obtain more information about this and your potential rights as a *qui tam* whistleblower at our website: http://www.justice.gov/sites/default/files/civil/legacy/2011/04/22/C-FRAUDS_FCA_Primer.pdf. If you would like to receive whistleblower funds, according to the law, you will need to file a qui tam action and be represented by an attorney.

Thank you again for contacting the Department. We hope the enclosed information is helpful.

Sincerely,

(Fig. 28 page 6)

From: Feedback, Civil
Sent: Wednesday, November 10, 2021 1:29 PM
To: Microsotf account team
Subject: RE: Qui Tam Whistleblower,

All mail is forwarded to the appropriate branches upon receipt. The answer to your question would depend upon the detail of your package which individual offices are not privy to due to the nature of the investigations themselves.

From: Microsotf account team <latellf@hotmail.com>
Sent: Thursday, November 04, 2021 3:41 PM
To: Feedback, Civil <cfeedbac@CIV.USDOJ.GOV>
Subject: [EXTERNAL] RE: Qui Tam Whistleblower,

Thank you, Communications Officer, Civil Division,

Can you tell me who the appropriate branch is?

Sincerely,

Frank Latell

Sent from Mail for Windows

From: Feedback, Civil
Sent: Thursday, November 4, 2021 8:35 AM
To: Microsotf account team
Subject: RE: Qui Tam Whistleblower,

Thank you, Mr. Latell,

Submitting documentation via U.S. mail is appropriate. Your mail was forwarded to the appropriate branch and appropriate action will be taken. Please keep in mind that we will be unable to comment further on any subsequent investigation.

We thank you for your time and understanding.

Sincerely,

Communications Office
Civil Division

From: Microsotf account team <latellf@hotmail.com>
Sent: Wednesday, November 03, 2021 10:33 AM

Chapter 40: Why Politicians are Disliked

After this last correspondence with the Department of Justice, I was hoping to get a boost from my government representatives. I sent the following letter with enclosures:

1. Copy of letter to U.S. Department of Justice, Office of Public Affairs (Fig. 27)

2. Email thread with the DOJ Civil Division (Fig. 28)

3. Short synopsis (Fig. 28)

4. My Story

(Fig. 29 page 1)

November 30, 2021

Frank Latell
5422 Peppertree Drive
Fort Myers, Florida 33908

Congressman Byron Donalds
523 Cannon HOB
Washington, DC 20515

USPS TRACKING # & CUSTOMER RECEIPT   **9114 9022 0078 9829 3190 04** For Tracking or inquiries go to USPS.com or call 1-800-222-1811.

Senator Marco Rubio
284 Russell Senate Office Building
Washington, DC 20510

USPS TRACKING # & CUSTOMER RECEIPT   **9114 9022 0078 9829 3185 19** For Tracking or inquiries go to USPS.com or call 1-800-222-1811.

Senator Rick Scott
716 Hart Senate Office Building
Washington, DC 20510

USPS TRACKING # & CUSTOMER RECEIPT   **9114 9022 0078 9829 3189 84** For Tracking or inquiries go to USPS.com or call 1-800-222-1811.

Enclosure: 1, copy of letter to U. S. Department of Justice, Office of Public Affairs
2, running dialog of my emails with the DOJ Civil Division
3, short synopsis
4, my story

Dear Congressman Donalds and Senators Rubio and Scott:

$150,000,000 (most likely more) was stolon from federal tax money through the bailout to Fannie Mae provided by the Housing Economic Recovery Act of 2008.

I spent many months trying to interest law firms and after becoming aware of the False Claims Act many more months concentrating on false claims act / qui tam whistleblower law firms. Although I've received responses that their firm could not or would not represent me, they have encouraged me to continue to pursue my claim and offered names of other law firms to contact.

(Fig. 29 page 2)

July 20, 2021, I sent a packet to the U. S. Department of Justice, Office of Public Affairs containing a forwarding letter (enclosure 1) along with enclosures 3 and 4. Upon not receiving a response I emailed civil.feedback@usdoj.gov. Enclosure 2, is my conversation with the DOJ Civil Division. The final email tells me that most likely my case has gone to the circular file.

The Federal Statute of Limitations is 10 years. The foreclosures of our properties took place in early 2012 although my court case was after that.

I respectfully hope that you will pursue this crime of stealing taxpayer money.

Sincerely,

Frank Latell
239 985 2260
latellf@hotmail.com

After four months of no response from my government representatives and knowing that they received my correspondence (tracking numbers), I knew that I needed to finish my story.

The proper ending to this book should be an investigation, a trial and a conviction. The fear and political connections kept this crime from being prosecuted. Fannie Mae and its co-conspirators, Santander Bank and Akerman Senterfitt are getting away with this scheme. The American taxpayer and I got screwed.

Epilogue

The conspiracy to steal millions or billions of taxpayer money was created by the US Governments authorization of unlimited bailout money to a lending institution, namely Fannie Mae. The servicer of Fannie Mae loans, namely Santander Bank, was allowed to offer millions of dollars of debt forgiveness for default borrowers to not interfere with foreclosure proceedings. Foreclosures were by a Fannie Mae attorney firm, namely Akerman Senterfitt, LLP, hired by the Fannie Mae loans servicer. Foreclosure sales properties were bought by Fannie Mae (high bidder) with direct title transfers from default borrowers to a subsidiary of Santander Bank, namely PBE Companies, LLC, or a ready buyer through a paper sale prior to the foreclosure.

One year of contacting attorneys who specialized in qui tam, false claim litigation proved non-productive, not because I did not have a case, but because of the challenges and fear of the power of the bailout conspirators.

The US Justice Department, who publicly welcomed whistleblowers, required nine requests of my complaint before I received a response. They informed me to get a lawyer to navigate the requirements of filing my complaint. Only upon my informing them that I've already spent $100,000 on lawyers did they respond that it is appropriate to file my complaint with them. They then informed me that they were sending my complaint to the appropriate branch and appropriate action would be taken, which I take to mean "the circular file."

Sending all information and assuming my government representatives would help to pressure the Justice Department to investigate my complaint resulted in no response.

This conspiracy to steal taxpayer money has been caught. Why is there a "too big to get away with crime" in this country? Why do politicians who swear an oath to protect the people's money pick and choose which criminals to give a pass? All men (and women) are equal, this crime needs to be resolved. Taxpayer money was stolen. Contact your Federal Government Representative and tell them to "get off their 'ass' and pursue this crime!"

I believe that in America "NO ONE IS ABOVE THE LAW." I've told my story; now it is up to the victims, you, to take action.

Reference List

Fig. 1 Affidavit of Frank Latell

Fig. 2 Kathleen and Frank Latell

Fig. 3 Croix Apartments

Fig. 4 Frank Latell

Fig. 5 Bethke Letter; June 13, 2011

Fig. 6 Agnew Letter to Rochefort; July 11, 2011

Fig. 7 Agnew Email Chain; July 14, 2011

Fig. 8 Frank Latell Letter to Rochefort via Agnew; July 24, 2011

Fig. 9 Carlus Flowers Letter; August 12, 2011

Fig. 10 Billboard

Fig. 11 Latell letter to the OCC; October 27, 2011

Fig. 12 Letter to Congress; January 7, 2013

Fig. 13 Third Amended Complaint; December 4, 2014

Fig. 14 Frank Latell Deposition

Fig. 15 Peppertree

Fig. 16 Peppertree Sale

Fig. 17 Triano's Transcript

Fig. 18 The old store

Fig. 19 Tony

Fig. 20 Matt Toll Letter; June 21, 2016

Fig. 21 Preface to Servicing Guide

Fig. 22 First Amended Complaint; November 2016

Fig. 23 CFPB Response; August 9, 2017

Fig. 24 CFPB Response; July 2, 2018

Fig. 25 FHFA Letter; December 30, 2011

Fig. 26 FHFA Letter; October 31, 2011

Fig. 27 Department of Justice Letter; July 20, 2021

Fig. 28 Department of Justice Civil Division and Frank Latell Email Thread

Fig. 29 Letter from Frank Latell to Senators Rubio and Scott and Congressman Donalds

Made in the USA
Middletown, DE
14 October 2023

40622058R00126